A REASON TO

A REASON TO Live

MELODY BEATTIE

GENERAL EDITOR

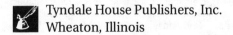

Tyndale House Publishers, Inc.
Wheaton, Illinois

Library of Congress Cataloging-in-Publication Data
A Reason to live / Melody Beattie, general editor.
     p.   cm.
  ISBN 0-8423-0988-8
    1. Suicide—Prevention. 2. Suicide–Psychological aspects.
3. Self-help techniques. 4. Helping behavior. 5. Suicide—
Religious aspects—Christianity. I. Beattie, Melody.
HV6545.R38 1991
362.2′87—dc20   91-14843

Printed in the United States of America

99 98 97 96 95 94 93 92 91
9   8   7   6   5   4   3   2

About the Contributors

Melody Beattie is the best-selling author of *Codependent No More; Beyond Codependency: And Getting Better All the Time;* and *The Language of Letting Go.* She lives in Minneapolis with her daughter and their new puppy. As the general editor for *A Reason to Live,* Melody contributed some of the material, was responsible for the selection of articles, and did the final organizing and editing of the book. Her enthusiasm, guidance, and input were the driving forces behind the project.

S. J. Anderson, a free-lance writer and speaker in the Washington, D.C., area, is the author of *When Someone Wants to Die* (Inter-Varsity, 1988), an account of her struggle with suicide. In addition to her written contributions to *A Reason to Live,* she also served as project consultant.

Other writers who have contributed to *A Reason to Live* are experienced in matters concerning suicide or have worked with those who are terminally ill. Many have themselves struggled with finding a reason to live. These writers (identified in the book by their initials) include Merrie Lee Bolesta, Marian Flandrick Bray, Tori Britton, Aneeta Brown, Susan Childress, Carl C. Dreizler, Betsy Rossen Elliot, Joyce K. Ellis, Sharon Fish, Jeron Frame, Melodie Schlenker Gage, Ruth Gordon, Joan Guest, Angela Elwell Hunt, Debra Jarvis, Lissa Halls Johnson, Timothy K. Jones, Debbie Kalmbach, Kent Keller, William P. Mahedy, Katherine L. Manchester, Kelsey Menehan, Connie Neal, Heidi K. Neff, Carole Gift Page, Randy Petersen, Judith Allen Shelly, Elizabeth R. Skoglund, Beth Lux Spring, Tim Stafford, Rayne Wagner, Wightman Weese, and Lance Wilcox.

CONTENTS

CHAPTER ONE

My Reason to Live

Every single day I wake up and I think of a reason not to do it. Every single day. ◆ Detective Riggs, after his wife died, in *Lethal Weapon*

*T*his is a book that explores reasons to live *and* reasons not to commit suicide. It also contains suggestions for life-affirming actions people can take to help themselves get through those times when they're struggling to find a reason to live.

For some people, ending their own lives—suicide—isn't an option.

For many others, it is. Five million living Americans have attempted to kill themselves, according to estimates from the American Association of Suicidology (AAS) in Denver, Colorado. In 1988, 30,407 succeeded. That's one person every 17.3 minutes.

These figures don't include unreported suicides, suicides that appeared to be accidental deaths, or the vast number of people who spend moments or months struggling through the process of considering, then rejecting, the idea of ending their own lives.

The AAS estimates that each suicide directly affects the lives of six other people. Based on these numbers, the AAS estimates that 3.5 million Americans have lost someone close to them to suicide, and this number grows by 180,000 each year.

Suicide rates in people ages fifteen to twenty-four have tripled in the last thirty years.

Who among us can forget the Jonestown, Guyana, suicide-massacre of 1978? Hundreds of men, women, and children followed the Reverend Jim Jones and his family through the doorway to death by drinking poisoned Kool-Aid. Hundreds more—who refused the sweet poison—were killed.

Who among us can forget learning about—or actually discovering—a friend or loved one hanged, overdosed on barbiturates, or shot through the head by his or her own hand?

I haven't been able to.

3

Suicide haunts. Devastates. And, sometimes, intrigues. The rocketing sales of *Final Exit,* a suicide manual written by Derek Humphrey, reflects a growing personal interest not only in euthanasia, but also, I believe, in suicide and death.

From the letters I receive almost daily from readers of my books, a large number of people are also passionately interested in another subject: life, living, and finding meaning in their lives.

A Reason to Live is a practical handbook for people who may be struggling to find a way, or a reason, to live.

It's for people who don't want to be here.

It's for people who don't consider suicide an option but wish they were dead.

It's for people considering suicide as an option and wondering if they should stick around.

It's for people who don't want to kill themselves but get trapped in suicidal thinking, or attempts, anyway.

And it's for people who want to kill themselves but wish someone could give them a reason to live.

It's also for people trying to give someone else—someone they know, love, or care about—a reason not to die *and* hope for life.

The book is a collection of articles written by authors across the nation. Some of these authors are professionals who counsel or help people haunted by the idea of suicide; some are people who have grappled with the idea personally. The alternatives to suicide are ideas that have worked either for them, or for people they know, or for their clients.

The reasons to live come from their hearts.

This is not a religious book, but it is spiritual. Some of the articles reflect the writers' religious beliefs, because to them—and to many others, including me—belief in a Higher Power, *God,* is at the top of the list of reasons to live and is intertwined with many others.

Tyndale House Publishers is an old friend of mine (they published my first book, written with Carolyn Owens). I agreed to edit this book when they called because I believed it was worthwhile and because I believed I could contribute professionally to the project.

But my reasons ran deeper. The request to work on this came at a crucial time in my life.

My head clamored, whirred, as I drove the van back from Breezy Point, a resort in northern Minnesota. It was summer 1991. My fourteen-year-old daughter, Nichole, and her three friends sat in the back playing card games, listening to music, singing.

This is a bad dream, I thought. It's just a really long, terrifying bad dream.

It started when I was three, maybe four, but it's just a dream, and I'm going to wake up. I want to open my eyes and have someone say, "Don't cry. Don't be afraid. It's not real. You're safe."

My mind flashed back to my childhood years. The sexual abuse. The rejection. The loneliness. A family that broke up when I was three and never got back together.

But that's OK, I thought. I survived it.

The drinking started at age twelve, the drinking that turned into alcoholism, then drug addiction. I flopped about in the drug culture, sticking needles in my arms until my veins disappeared. Then, an unplanned pregnancy. Having a baby. Frantically getting married so my son wouldn't be illegitimate. The separation.

Losing the custody suit.

I remember sitting in my attorney's office, taking the hand of my three-year-old son, John, walking him halfway across the hallway, letting the other attorney take his hand to lead him away from me.

Years of grief, pain, guilt, and remorse.

Watching friends die. Not caring if I died. Wishing I was dead. Overdoses, time after time, landed me in the critical care unit of the general hospital of whichever city I was in . . . until one day I landed in front of a judge who gave me a choice: treatment or jail.

The car ride to treatment. Not wanting to be there. Sitting on the lawn one day. Remembering, realizing, that God is . . . and that God is real. I don't know if I found him or he found me.

Eight months later I walked out the door. I was scared, determined, committed: to God, sobriety, and a new life.

My ex-fiancé overdosed on drugs. I met a new man—a respected man with seven years' sobriety. We fell in love, got married. At last I had it all.

I got pregnant. Nichole. A beautiful baby daughter. I wanted another. I wanted a family—finally, at last, and forever. I wanted a son. Beautiful, loving Shane was born.

I started my career as a writer.

Marriage is falling apart. Husband is a practicing alcoholic. I love my kids, but I'm going crazy. What's wrong? What's wrong? What's wrong? I'm trying to do everything right. I'm sober. I'm trying to make my husband stop drinking. I never get angry. I always help other people.

And my life is falling apart and I wish I were dead and I don't know why. Dear God, I don't know why.

I learn why: a problem called *codependency*. I divorce my husband, go on welfare, and write a book about it. The book gets published. I forget about it. No book will ever change my life, I think. I write because I love to write, not because I want to make money.

I work for the newspaper, struggle financially, hope to make ends meet.

No matter what, the kids and I have each other. We have love. We are a family. No matter what.

The book takes off. Hits the best-seller list. My life changes. Money. Success. More work.

New clothes for the children, for the first time in their lives. New clothes for me, for the first time in my life. A car that runs. No more bill collectors.

And enough contracts to keep me writing the rest of my life.

In July 1990, I call a halt to the writing. Something tells me to stop, to take time, to spend all my time with the children. Shane asks to go to the Virgin Islands. We go. Shane and Nichole ask to go to Breezy Point. We go.

We go to movies. We watch television. We spend so much time together that the children beg for "less family bonding time." I *can't* stop myself.

"No," I say. "We're going to do more."

Wednesday: Shane's family birthday dinner, on January 30. He's twelve. And proud of it. I make him and Nichole promise that no matter where we are, or how old we are, we'll always get together for dinner on our birthdays. The look in Shane's eyes haunts me.

He keeps bugging me, bugging me, bugging me, about the title of one of my recent books, *The Language of Letting Go*.

"What's the name of that book?" he asks at least thirty times.

Thursday: Shane digs through my jewelry box and asks if he can have my ornate gold cross. I say yes, wondering about the request.

Friday: Shane pulls down his sweater collar and shows me the cross hanging from a chain around his neck. He looks in my eyes and says, "God is with me now."

Saturday: I get the call. "Your son has been knocked unconscious on the ski slopes. Don't worry, it happens all the time. We'll call back."

The next call, fifteen minutes later. "Shane is in an ambulance on the way to the hospital. You'd better meet him there."

The drive to the hospital.

"I'm Melody Beattie, and I'm supposed to meet my son here. Where is he?"

The look in their eyes. "Do you want to call a chaplain?"

Brain-dead. How could he be brain-dead?

"We have to turn the respirator off, Mrs. Beattie. His kidneys are backing up. His brain is dead."

"NO!" I scream. "NO!"

"I believe in miracles. I believe in God. I believe in hope. There's always hope."

"No, Melody. This time, there is no hope."

I call my best friend. She comes. Other people come. Fifty people come. They hold my hand, hold my daughter's hand.

Pastor Dave comes. Pray about it, I say. Talk to God. Get me a miracle. I'll do anything. But don't take my baby away. Please. I tell him I'll surrender, but only if I have to.

Dave goes into a room. Prays. Reads the Bible. Comes out, looking down, shaking his head.

I hold Shane in my arms. I say good-bye, I love you, I'll always love you. I cut a lock of his hair. Someone turns off the respirator. Shane exhales the air in his lungs. He doesn't breathe any more in.

The wake. The funeral.

Balloons. So many brightly colored balloons. The February sky in Minneapolis is bright and blue. We celebrate Shane's life in the chapel. Then we each hold a balloon and, together, we let go. We release his spirit.

Nichole and I move to Minneapolis. We look at each other, wondering where our family went, wondering where all the men went.

Day after day, we get through. I go through the motions. I cry. There's a hole in my heart. It hurts. It hurts a lot. I wake up in the morning, go to movies, work a little. Nichole cries. And I cry.

Friends surround us. The man I've been dating stands by my side. "But not forever," he says, crawling into that grim hole called "I love my freedom and independence."

No commitment.

A feeling, an impulse, nags at me, pushes me to the hospital, to visit the mother of a friend of Nichole's and Shane's. Eight years before, in the process of fighting Hodgkin's, she developed leukemia. Now the chemotherapy she endured to give her a few more years of life has destroyed her body. The bone marrow transplant, despite her determination and faith in God, hasn't worked.

I walk in hours after she comes out of delirium. She looks at me and her friend, sitting in the room with us. "I'm ready to die now," she says. "I'm going to go to heaven. I'm going to see Shane. I'm going to be with God."

Two days later, she dies.

I envy her. I love Nichole, but I feel divided—like a woman who has one child on each side of the river.

Now, another weekend at Breezy Point. Same time, one year

later. Different people. I take the boat to the island, looking, searching. Shane isn't there. I look at Nichole—grieving, frightened. She has lost her best friend.

Can't let her lose her mother, too.

I remember her words. They echo through my head. I had to fly somewhere. She was scared the plane would crash. I tried to reassure her. "Just ask God to protect me," I said. "And he'll keep me safe."

"Just like he did with Shane?" she asked.

It is a bad dream. A terrible dream. A long, terrible dream. And I want to wake up.

I feel like Ettie Mae Green, reportedly the oldest woman in the world. She sleeps for three days, then stays up for three days.

"It's been a pretty good life, I guess," she told *Minneapolis Star Tribune* writers. "I'm so tired I can hardly stand it."

Always before, I have found strength, faith, determination, courage, hope. I have gotten knocked down, but I have come back. Now, I am tired.

Nichole has lost her brother. We have lost our family structure, as we knew it. I have lost my son. But I have lost even more than that.

I have lost a big part of my reason to live.

When we got home from the trip, I called a friend. "I'm really upset," I said. "Something's going on with me."

"What's that?" she asked.

"I'm realizing that I really don't want to be here."

She knew about my life; she knew about Shane's death. She listened for a moment, then replied, "Of course you don't. Who would *want* to go through what you're going through?

"But you'll feel better, soon."

"Imagine this," I told another friend. "You're holding a loaded gun to your head, trigger cocked. 'Give me a reason to live!' you say."

(My friend had been through his moments of despair. I figured he was a good subject for this experiment.)

"So I tell you to count your blessings, do volunteer work, and be grateful for your pain and suffering. What would you do?" I asked.

"Probably shoot you first, then myself next," he answered.

"Is there anything I could do that might change your mind about living?" I asked.

"Yeah," he replied, after a long silence. "Take the gun away from me, point it at my head, and tell me *you're* going to kill me."

While this might work for many people, it wouldn't work for all. Some of us do have those times when we'd stand there, go limp, and say "Go ahead. Pull the trigger. Please. Do me and everyone else a favor."

And we'd mean it.

(Incidentally, this is not a suggestion. It's an illustration. If anyone picks up and aims a gun, loaded or unloaded, *leave* and call 911.)

My biggest fear about working on this book was that the reasons to live would sound trite, trivial. Something bothered me about the reasons to live, and I wasn't sure what it was.

Clarity wasted little time coming, once I recognized my fear. Ironically, part of my answer came from a movie. (Yes, movies are high on my list of "Immediate Life-Affirming Alternatives." I have sat through many barely able to decipher what was being said or why I was there.)

In the movie *City Slickers*, Mitch—a disgruntled husband and father—decides to go to a dude ranch. Mid-life crisis has hit, and life doesn't seem to have much meaning. He hopes he can find some there.

His answer comes from Curly, a surly old cowboy who complains about city slickers spending fifteen years getting "knots in their rope," then expecting two weeks at the dude ranch to untie those knots.

"Do you know what the secret of life is?" Curly asks Mitch.

"No, what?" Mitch says.

"This," Curly says, holding up one finger.

"Your finger?" Mitch asks.

"One thing, just one thing," Curly says.

"That's great, but what's the one thing?" Mitch asks.

"That's what *you* gotta figure out," Curly says.

That dialogue perplexed me. It perplexed Mitch, too. Later in the movie, when a happy Mitch returned to his wife and children, it was clear he had figured it out.

That confused me even more.

What could that one thing be? Why didn't they give the answer? Working on this project, I got the answer. That's why I was apprehensive about what I offered to people, and whether they would accept *our* list of reasons.

Mitch and Curly were talking about the same thing we are in this book: a reason to live. And nobody can give you that. It is the struggling for, searching for, then discovering and embracing of it that makes *a* reason to live *your* reason to live.

People can make suggestions. People can tell you, as best they're able to articulate, what their reason for living is. But I can't give you mine; you can't give me yours. It won't work. It isn't ours until we find it and make it ours—or until it finds us.

It may also be that different elements or ideas contribute to, shape, and form that reason. And it may be that the reason shifts and changes over the years, adapting to different seasons in our lives.

Sometimes it never forms, if conditions in our childhood don't nurture and shape it. Sometimes when we are adults it gets shaken to the core—blown out, blown away, shattered. Many of us don't think about or define our reason to live until we find ourself without one—or at least without one we can recognize.

During my transition from not wanting to be here to making a commitment to being here with peace, from meaningless to meaning, from feeling doomed to die anyway to realizing I was full of life, I was lucky. I was surrounded by people who loved me, accepted me, and didn't try to "fix" me or make me be or feel something I wasn't or didn't.

They worried, I'm sure. But mostly they loved me, supported me, and helped guide me through.

I was also lucky enough to have a God that hung in with me through my rage, through endless days of being too despairing to pray or to make conscious contact with him. When I couldn't talk, he still heard me. When I didn't know what I needed, he did.

I hope you will find the same through the days, months, and years ahead as you discover, and embrace, your reason to live.

CHAPTER TWO

Immediate Alternatives

C ry. Laugh. Go to a movie.

Take a bath. Take a walk. Exercise. Call a friend.

These are not necessarily reasons to live, but they are things to do while we're finding one. They are things to do that can help us feel better and move toward our goal instead of away from it.

People attribute many reasons to suicide. The purpose of this book is not to explore or define those reasons. But I believe that part of the desire to kill ourself is a deep desire—despite the unknowns we have about heaven and the afterlife—to have just one moment of control over our life during times when we feel powerless.

Suicide is an option, but there are other options that can also give you one moment of control. You can use your creative ability and power to choose by making a choice that affirms life.

The suggestions in this section are ideas that you can implement now. Today. Read through the list, and find some that appeal to you. If none appeal, make yourself do one or more of them anyway.

Or create a positive suggestion of your own.

You'll know what to do, what feels right for you and your circumstances.

Here are some things I did—and still do—that help.

Talk it out. This is important. I had to talk and talk and talk. Even when I didn't want to. When I started sliding into blackness, I had usually stopped expressing myself.

I talked to other people a lot. Sometimes, I sat in front of the mirror and talked to myself. There was something validating about this; I could do it any time of the day or night, and it was really hard to lie to myself about what I was feeling and thinking. It gave me an opportunity to fully express all those things I felt awkward blurting out to someone.

A word of caution: I only did this when someone was around or available to support me if I got into some powerful feelings.

One of the ideas that was helpful to me was the one about getting mad at God. One day, I went to the cemetery and yelled at God. I told God how I felt about what had happened. I told God what I needed. And then I had to forgive myself for getting angry, because although part of me knew it was OK to express myself with God that way, another part needed my forgiveness.

Other things I did included wearing lighter colors. The night before Shane died, the last contingency had been removed on purchasing the new house Nichole and I moved to. I got a geographical lift, which helped me. The other house made my heart ache. Seeing the school bus pull up at two-thirty each day, and not seeing Shane get off, made my heart ache.

The new house was a gift. It was light and airy. Lots of sunlight. Lots of white walls. But I was wearing black—every day. One day I decided: that's enough. Black looked good on me. But just as sunlight and light rooms lightened my mood, so did the colors I wore.

I'd feel depressed if I sat in a black room. Wearing black wasn't helping me much either. I put my black clothes away, until I felt better.

I went for walks. I got out in nature, even if that meant sitting in the backyard.

Get outside. Look at the trees, the flowers. Watch the birds. Take time to notice the insects too. Try to get near water—a lake, a stream, a brook. If you can't physically get outdoors, open the window or have someone rent a nature tape for you to watch. Let nature tell its story to you.

Music helps. I listened to "Life Is Eternal" by Carly Simon and "Unchained Melody" by the Righteous Brothers more than a hundred times. Over and over, I played the music, letting it wash through me. Music with a faster beat can invigorate you, get you moving when you feel sluggish.

Find something to do, then do it. Reading the list won't do it. Thinking about the list won't do it. Take action. Choose one thing, then make yourself do it.

Yes, feeling our feelings is important, critical, and healthy. But it's good to distract ourself, too. It's good to know that we don't have to let our feelings control us.

Help yourself feel better today.

Call a suicide prevention hotline.

☀ Help is as close as the nearest telephone.

Maybe it looks as if there are no sources of help for you. Treatment is too expensive; you can't afford the time away from your job; there are no appropriate facilities near you; you are too ashamed to talk to someone you know. You don't know where to turn.

Telephone!

If you are depressed, suicidal, or abusing drugs or alcohol, the professional crisis counselors of the National Suicide Prevention Hotline are available to speak to you, personally and confidentially.

Do there seem to be no resources in your area? There *is* help for you, and the people at suicide prevention hotlines know where and how to find it.

Is lack of money a problem? The counselors who answer the phones will direct you to help you can afford—or will find ways to cover the expense of the help you need.

Are you pressed for time? You can phone 24 hours a day, 365 days a year. The National Suicide Prevention Hotline always has counselors at the telephones.

Call. You are not bothering anyone! That's why they're there. CN

The National Suicide Prevention Hotline's number is 1-800-333-4444. There may also be a local hotline in your area. Check the white pages under Suicide Prevention.

Make a life pact with someone.

✳ News media quickly jump on stories if there's even a hint that there was a suicide pact involved. It's high drama, but what a waste! Why not protect yourself and create your own private high drama by making a life pact with someone instead?

If you have ever been so despondent that you have considered taking your life, find someone in your family, workplace, neighborhood, or church with whom you can be honest. As hard as it may be, tell them what you have been contemplating and ask them to enter into a life pact with you—that neither of you will take your own life without first talking to the other one about it.

"I had the pills in my hand, ready to swallow them. The pact I had made with Carolyn instantly came to mind. I put them down and called her instead," said Andrea. Find someone who will agree with you that life is worth living, then write your pact and sign it.

You might not think your friend has any suicidal thoughts, but you don't know what has been going on in that person's mind or what seemingly insurmountable problems he or she may face in the days ahead. Your opening up to someone else may save that person's life, too. JKE

If you don't feel comfortable talking about this with anyone you know, call a suicide hotline in your area or this national number: 1-800-333-4444. Make a life pact with a counselor by phone.

Take a walk.

☀ My chronic illness dictates that I'm on at least one medication and sometimes several at once. Unfortunately, they have
strong side effects. One of the effects is depression. Depression as
in I-want-to-kill-myself-where-are-the-knives?

If I can force myself to go for a walk, I often begin to feel a little
better. Sometimes just stepping outside into the cool wind helps.
For me, walking for a half hour or an hour makes me less
depressed. And I sleep better at night, so I'm not wandering about
at weird hours thinking black thoughts.

Exercise does alter your body. Your blood and oxygen circulate
faster and invigorate you. Endorphins are secreted by the brain;
this relaxes you and calms you down. When you're done exercising, you're pleasantly tired. I always feel as if I've accomplished at
least one good thing in the day when I take a walk.

Sometimes I walk a couple of miles on the track near my house.
Lots of other people are there, too. I like to watch them and not
feel so alone.

Walking helps push back the heavy cloud of depression. MFB

*Go for a walk. If you don't like walking, do another exercise you like.
Borrow a bike. Treat yourself to an hour of horseback riding. Swim
in a friend's pool. Shoot some baskets with a neighbor's child. Turn
on the radio and move to the music.*

Give yourself twenty-four hours.

The late Catherine Marshall once said she believed that most people who commit suicide would not do so if they just waited for twenty-four hours. Time heals. Time gives us a chance to put things into perspective. Time gives us the opportunity to reach out for help.

Before you exit, hang tough a little longer. See if things look better. Wait, and you still have options. Exit, and your options are gone.

On July 4, 1952, Florence Chadwick pushed off from Catalina Island and began the long swim toward the California coast. Several men had already conquered the twenty-one-mile channel, but no women. Chadwick had already swum the English Channel in both directions. If any woman could do it, she could.

For almost sixteen hours her will battled the numbing waters, fog, and sharks. Finally, still in heavy fog and unsure how much further she had to go, she asked to be pulled from the water. Hours later she learned how close she had come: she was only a half mile from the California shore.

If people, events, and life have left you in a fog, don't give in. Hang in a little longer. You may be closer to shore than you think.

(Two months later, Chadwick tried again. The second time, despite cold, fatigue, sharks, and fog, she made it, breaking the men's record by two hours.)

Sometimes, time won't change the circumstance causing our distress. But even one day may alter our perspective, our emotions, or our resolve to see the circumstance through. KK/ERS

A decision to die is a permanent one. Don't die on impulse. Even if you've thought it out, wait. Call one more friend. Check with one more doctor. Call a hotline (the Suicide Prevention Hotline is 1-800-333-4444). Change is certain; so is the prospect of transformation.

Yell "Fire!"

✳ Years ago the Smothers Brothers did a comedy routine called "Chocolate." Tommy, the younger and supposedly dumber brother, began a little song in which he said that he had fallen into a vat of chocolate.

His brother, Dick, repeated the tune, asking what Tommy did when he fell into the chocolate.

Tommy sang back that he yelled, "Fire!"

Why "Fire"? asked Dick.

Tommy answered, "Because nobody would have rescued me if I had yelled 'Chocolate!'"

Try yelling "Fire!" when you've fallen into something you can't handle. Not literally, of course. You can get arrested for yelling "Fire!" in a public place. But try letting someone else know that you're in real danger.

Many of us get so busy with our own schedules and difficulties that we don't hear those around us who are trying to tell us they're in trouble. We're not trying to be insensitive. Everyone has problems, we think. And it's hard to know when someone has gotten to that point of desperation. We need to be told, plainly and directly.

Try opening up to someone you trust. Let them know how serious the problems have become. Don't be subtle. Don't hint. If necessary, exaggerate to get their attention.

Yell "Fire!" because no one will know you need to be rescued if you yell "Chocolate!" JKE

For help in learning to open up to others, read Why Am I Afraid to Tell You Who I Am? *by John Powell (Tabor Publ.). If you need a friend who will listen, call The Befrienders Ministry (1-800-328-6819, ext. 5095), an ecumenical program with information about someone near you who* wants *to listen.*

Surround yourself with flowers.

Several years ago, as part of an advertising campaign, a florist mailed calendars to many of its customers. I still remember the motto at the top, in swirling black letters: "You can live without flowers—but not very well."

Some people like to take naps, others prefer to go fishing. Some like to work in the garden. But most of us, even those who have no green thumb, enjoy looking at fresh flowers.

Pink or red roses, yellow and purple daisies, peach-colored gladiolus. Honeysuckles, lilies of the valley, mums, and wild violets. Each offers a unique combination of beauty, fragrance, and color.

Flowers help heal the heart.

Don't wait for someone to send you flowers; get some for yourself. Pick some; buy some; keep them close by. AB

Spend at least one hour strolling through a greenhouse.

Make yourself laugh.

The flip side of tragedy is comedy.

In his essay on Hamlet and King Lear, Coleridge noted that "the grimace of mirth resembles the grimace of suffering; comic and tragic masks have the same distortion."

Yet, Coleridge continued, "comedy seems to be a more pervasive human condition than tragedy." Despite its serious disappointments, life is also full of humor.

And humor heals.

When *Saturday Review* publisher Norman Cousins learned he had a terminal illness, he made the decision to live, not die. If medical treatment had no answers for him, then he would devise his own therapy. Mr. Cousins's highly unconventional program included watching funny movies for hours at a time—The Three Stooges, "Candid Camera," Laurel and Hardy. Immersed in comedy, he began to laugh. The more he laughed, the better he felt. The better he felt, the more encouraging his lab tests turned out.

Although humor may not "cure" your problem, it can help you feel better—now.

Why does laughter make us feel better? Researchers have many theories—laughter speeds up the heart, exercises the muscles, fortifies the immune system, reduces the effects of stress, releases endorphins (natural painkillers) into the system . . .

Remember a time when you laughed out loud. Remember how good it felt?

Let yourself laugh. In fact, make yourself laugh. Humor can save your life. SJA

Today, go to your nearest video store and rent your favorite comedy. One suggestion: Trains, Planes and Automobiles *starring John Candy and Steve Martin. Or go to a movie billed as a comedy. Or go to the library and check out a book by Erma Bombeck or Dave Barry.*

Get mad at God.

I've gotten really mad about my bad health and lousy circumstances. At first I would try to blame others. Then I realized that ultimately God was the one responsible. He was the only one in charge, the only one who could change things. But he often chose not to. That steamed me good.

Friends have told me I shouldn't get mad at him, but if he's my heavenly Father then I can tell him what I'm thinking. It's OK to be mad at God. He can take it.

Sometimes I'd be so mad that I'd want to actually hit him if I could. I'd tell him over and over how enraged I was at the state of my life, most of it out of control, stuff I was helpless to change.

Suppressing anger can make you sicker or more depressed, so venting your anger in a controlled manner is good.

As I continued to tell God I was mad at him, things began to change. Unfortunately it wasn't my circumstances. I am still sick. But somehow yelling my prayers at him helped me to become more accepting of things I had no power over. Not that I was a doormat, but I began to pause and glance around for alternatives. Maybe I didn't always have to get my own way to be happy.

Bringing my anger to God helped me to feel better. MFB

Read the poem "Do Not Go Gentle into That Good Night" by Dylan Thomas, a twentieth-century Welsh poet. A librarian can help you find it. The poem talks about the poet's intense anger about death.

Cry.

The suicide rate for men is four times that of women. One reason may be the frequent inability of men to express their deepest needs and feelings.

Hang tough. Big boys don't cry. Many little boys have learned from their fathers the manly art of stifling grief. But men *and* women have reasons to cry.

An example is Ed Miller. Ed's wife of forty-five years died unexpectedly. Ed stopped going to visit friends, stopped going anywhere.

A woman befriended him, and he accepted. He invited Sharon over for lunch and talked about the weather, his garden, and the latest book he read. But he never talked about his wife. Ed never cried, never grieved.

Several months passed and Ed still stayed at home. He was tired and wanted to be alone.

One day Sharon dropped by Ed's house to give him a book about grief and loss. He told her he wouldn't read it, but she left it on the table anyway. Three days later she received a phone call. Ed was laughing, crying, and shouting at the same time. "I'm normal! Thank you!"

Grieving is a normal part of life. We have tear ducts for a reason. Crying can release fear, hurt, and despair. It can help unfold rage. It's healthy to cry when you need to; it's OK to let others *see* you cry. In fact, it may help give them permission to feel their feelings.

What we don't feel *can* hurt us. It can make us tired, withdrawn, confused. It can kill us. Crying can help cleanse pain from the heart and soul.

Try crying, even—especially—if you don't like it. SF/LHJ

If you have trouble crying, try reading a sad book or watching a sad movie.

Cry for ten minutes.

When life gets so unbearable that we no longer want to live, one common denominator—despite our individual circumstances—is the presence of emotions that appear out of control. They may be stored from a whole lifetime; they may be triggered by a current event. Or both.

We were all brought up differently. In some homes emotions are ignored, or even punished. To survive, we may have learned to be emotionally cold. As many experts have stated, unfelt emotions can control our lives. Feelings need to be felt and released. Crying is one way to do that.

Some of us have a difficult time squeezing out one tear; some of us—once we learn to cry—can't stop crying.

If it's difficult for you to control your tears, if you cry for hours at a time, consider allowing yourself a ten-minute crying session once or twice a day. Set an alarm clock, or ask a friend to call you when ten minutes have passed.

If crying is difficult for you, try forcing tears for ten minutes. It may feel like an eternity, but keep at it. Make sure you have something scheduled—even a minor distraction—when the ten minutes end. It will help you move on until your next scheduled cry.

It's healthy to feel our feelings, but helpful to know we don't have to let them control us. CCD

Keep a list of the things that make you sad. Cry about them in your next scheduled ten-minute session. The rest of the day, do your best to cope.

Pray the Serenity Prayer.

✳ Life can, at times, seem like an overwhelming combination of pressures. Some are within our control; some are way beyond it. A brief prayer, written by the theologian Reinhold Niebuhr, cuts to the heart of our need: "God, grant me the serenity to accept the things I cannot change, the courage to change the things I can, and the wisdom to know the difference."

In the Serenity Prayer we address God as God, the One who knows us, accepts us, and is waiting and willing to hear from us.

Then we ask him for serenity, for we need a calm to accept those things beyond our ability to change—a downturn in the economy, another person's anger, our own physical limitations, the loss of a loved one. This is not the bitter resignation we may often feel but rather the acceptance of a situation—acceptance that can bring both rest and the possibility of other solutions.

Next, we request courage both to face and to change those many things that we *are* able to change—most especially our own attitudes, actions, and reactions.

At times the line between what is and is not our responsibility is far from clear—for example, when another's actions have significant consequences for us and it is not obvious whether accepting a situation or attempting to change it is the better course. This is where the last phrase of the prayer applies—asking for wisdom. We may need patience to wait for the wisdom, but eventually it will come.

We needn't feel overwhelmed by problems or paralyzed by inaction. God is listening. BRE

Memorize the Serenity Prayer phrase by phrase. Write it on a small card and carry it with you. Make each phrase your own, meditating on one at a time while you're learning it. Then ask God for serenity, courage, and wisdom by praying it as you go—while walking, at bedtime, during your commute to work or school, wherever you go.

Go to a children's bookstore.

✳ In the world of television commercials, a certain rabbit has been trying for years to get a bowl of a certain breakfast cereal. Alas, he is always detected and admonished with the words, "Silly rabbit! Trix are for kids."

Some of us may think of children's books in the same way. If we take a peek at one, we expect some parental voice to tell us to grow up and read a more respectable book (preferably without pictures). Don't trick yourself into believing that children's books are just for kids.

Go to a children's bookstore or a good-sized children's section of a larger store. Give yourself plenty of time to browse through the shelves. Visit your old favorites—you'll find that *Goodnight Moon* is still tucking little folks into bed, Dr. Seuss's wacky rhymes and outrageous characters are still bringing smiles to our face, Beverly Cleary's and Katherine Paterson's youngsters are still voicing the questions and doubts of many, and the Chronicles of Narnia and Frank Baum's Oz books are still whisking readers away to other worlds.

But there's also a crop of new and exciting books with peekaboo windows and pop-up features and textured pages. There are new, beautiful illustrations that make us marvel. And anybody can read and enjoy them, no matter how old he or she is.

Go ahead, reach for Daniel Pinkwater's *Guys from Space* or Maurice Sendak's *Where the Wild Things Are* or Margery Williams's *Velveteen Rabbit*. Silly adult! Books are for all us kids! BRE

Visit a children's bookstore. Buy something for the child in you—a new edition of a childhood favorite or whatever catches your eye. Then buy something for a child you know.

Cast yourself in *It's a Wonderful Life.*

✳ From Thanksgiving through Christmas, you'll find Frank
Capra's classic movie *It's a Wonderful Life* replayed many
times.

George Bailey, played by Jimmy Stewart, contemplates committing suicide on Christmas Eve because he faces financial ruin and
believes his life has been a waste. An angel, Clarence, is dispatched
to earth to show George how valuable his life has been by showing
him what his hometown, Bedford Falls, and his family and friends
would be like had he never been born.

Sometimes, we may feel it would be better if we'd never been
born. We believe our life is without meaning.

Take time out and think about the good and worthwhile things
you've done—starting in childhood: the people you reached out
to, the large and small accomplishments that made a difference.
Count your intentions, too—the times you cared (even if nobody
noticed), the times you tried to love people.

Don't minimize what you've done, or discount something that
was part of a team effort. Don't minimize the importance of small
acts of kindness: those people you touched by smiling and saying
hi each day.

Maybe you gave someone hope or a reason to live, even if you
weren't aware of it—by needing them, or allowing them to need
you.

Whoever you are, and whatever your path has been, *you made a
difference.* The world would not be the same without you. BRE

Rent and watch the movie It's a Wonderful Life. *Cast yourself in the
lead role and consider the difference your life has made. Don't be
afraid to experience the joy George Bailey felt when he saw how
much he meant to others.*

Listen to music.

Music has the power to express a mood, create a mood, transform your mood. Music can soothe and uplift.

The dramatic scene in a movie that keeps you on the edge of your chair can be sterile and so-so without the soundtrack. Or you can watch the same scene five times, with the music turned on, and still be gripped—even though you know what's going to happen next.

Do sad songs make us sad? Sometimes. But do happy songs make us happy? Not if the lyrics seem to mock our strained emotions. The power of music to transform and uplift our mood is recognizable and immediate—as long as it is the right music for us at the right time.

What is the *right* music? It may be a symphony by Beethoven, a cassette tape by Yanni, or a rendition of *When You Wish upon a Star.* Choose the best from classical, contemporary, oldies, gospel songs, and spirituals.

Randy was twelve when his mother died after a lingering illness. His father had abandoned him when he was three. He was at a friend's home one evening, about a month after his mother's death. A guest in the home was playing the guitar and singing to the children. Suddenly, Randy grabbed his friend and whispered in his ear, "Please ask her to play the 'Amazing Grace' song again."

Randy had tears in his eyes. It was the first time he had cried in months.

Music can help express your mood and longings, and leave you on higher ground when the song ends. BRE/KLM

Dedicate twenty minutes every other day to listening to music. Experiment. Go through your records; check music out at the library; listen to the radio. Try a different station than you normally choose; try different types of music than you usually choose. When the music has words, sing along.

Soak up some sunshine.

✳ Beth, played by Jessica Lange in Warner Brothers' *Men Don't Leave,* closed the curtains and took to her bed. Months before, her husband had died in an accident. After losing him and her home and struggling to raise two sons without their father, she could no longer pretend to be strong. She refused to answer the door and ate spaghetti out of the can when she was hungry.

Beth's turning point came, some two weeks later, when her son's girlfriend, Jody (played by Joan Cusack), barged into Beth's bedroom, opened the blinds, and forced her out of bed, into the shower, and then outdoors for a surprise: a hot-air balloon ride.

When we're depressed, it's tempting to sleep a lot and to close the drapes during the daytime to enable ourselves to sleep. But when we do, we block out one good resource to help ourselves feel better: the sun.

You may not want to go for a balloon ride, but you can throw open the drapes. Make excuses for yourself—if you have to—to get outside and soak up the sunshine.

Try sitting in the sun to read, to dry your hair after your shower, or to work on a hobby. Eat outside on your lunch hour; try walking instead of driving for short errands.

Take a dose of vitamin D directly from its source. JKE/KLM

Is there a pattern to your depression? Do you feel all right in the summer but terrible in the winter? If you think your problem is related to winter doldrums (called seasonal affective disorder), ask your physician, a psychologist, or a counselor for help. There are ways to solve this common problem.

Tell your secret to someone who will understand.

It was in all the newspapers—a little girl we will call Stephanie had been abducted from a shopping mall in Southern California. Her foster parents reported that she had disappeared while the whole family was shopping at the mall.

The search began immediately. Pictures of Stephanie with her shy smile and pleading brown eyes were posted everywhere. A few weeks later, newspapers reported that the police were closing in on their prime suspect.

When confronted by the police, Stephanie's foster father confessed to the killing. There had been no abduction at the mall. Discipline had gotten out of hand and had turned into abuse.

Shortly after confessing, Stephanie's foster father hung himself.

Had abuse been a regular part of Stephanie's life? The newspapers didn't say. It is, however, a dark secret in hundreds of thousands of homes across this country, and it may well have been a secret in Stephanie's foster home too.

What if Stephanie's foster father had told a close friend that he was having trouble controlling his anger? What if he had asked for help in disciplining Stephanie in a way that would not hurt her?

What if Stephanie had told her social worker that she was being mistreated?

What if Stephanie's foster mother had confided in someone about the family tensions?

Perhaps two people would not have had to die. CN

If you don't have a friend to confide in, try the Childhelp USA Child Abuse Hotline at 1-800-422-4453. Another source of help is Parents Anonymous at 1-800-421-0353. They offer free anonymous consultation, professional help, and support relating to parenting issues, including child abuse.

Talk to a clergy member.

☀ Most clergy genuinely care about people and want to help in any way they can. They are seldom shocked. Helping people deal with anger, guilt, illness, hopelessness, and despair is part of their job. But often they are the last to know when a member of their church is considering suicide.

We usually want the minister to see us in the best light, so we cover up our problems and act as if everything is fine. Then we get angry because he or she doesn't offer to help. Or we may feel that the minister couldn't do anything to change the situation anyway, so why bother him or her. But a pastor can help in several ways.

First, the pastor can be there for you. Even when you feel no one else will listen or care, he or she will. Sometimes just being able to discuss your feelings with someone will help put your struggles into perspective.

Second, pastors are trained to hear confessions. Often the root of depression is a deep anger against ourselves for something we are sure God cannot forgive. Confession and assurance of forgiveness can begin the healing process.

Finally, the minister usually knows and cares for other members of your family. Many struggles that lead to suicidal thoughts involve family dynamics that need changing. A clergy person can refer you to a competent professional counselor and support you and your family in the recovery process. JAS

If you do not know a pastor to call, a ministerial association or a pastoral counseling center can recommend one. Try the white pages of your phone book. Look up either your county's or city's name, followed by the word ministerial *or* pastoral. *If that leads nowhere, try phoning churches that have display ads in the yellow pages.*

Get a good night's sleep.

Nancy recently said, "Before I started my vacation, I just couldn't handle my bills. I felt overwhelmed. After a few days of rest and recreation, somewhere in the middle of the week, I remembered that stack of bills. Suddenly, I realized things weren't as bad as I had thought."

When Nancy was exhausted, her tight budget made life seem overwhelming. The budget was still tight; that hadn't changed. But with rest, the impossible became possible.

A lot of exhausted, hopeless people simply need, before anything else, a good night's sleep. A psychiatrist observed, "Put a group of students in a room, deprive them of sleep for three days, and you will have people who see pink elephants or feel that people are poisoning them. They develop psychotic symptoms. The cure is just plain rest."

Here's a story about sleep:

Elijah the prophet was burned out. He wanted to die. "I've had enough," he told God. "Take away my life. I've got to die sometime. Why not now?" Elijah lay down and went to sleep, hoping God would let him die. Instead, an angel came, fed him, and allowed him to go back to sleep. And Elijah went on to finish his task.

During times of grief or duress, we may need more sleep than usual. Our body needs the energy we usually expend in living to process the intense emotions and stress. If we're draining ourselves by keeping too busy and not getting enough sleep, we deplete one good natural resource for healing—ourselves.

Get a good night's sleep. In fact, get ten hours of sleep when you need it. Maybe the angels will come to help us, too. ERS

Go sailing or to the beach. Do something that helps you relax. Take a hot bath and read a good novel before bed to help you forget the day and sleep. Recharge your batteries before you go back to work.

Do two things each day.

✳ In times of severe crisis, when you don't want to do anything, do two things each day. Depending on your physical and emotional condition, the two things could be taking a shower and making a phone call (getting dressed is included in taking a shower), or writing a letter and painting a room.

Writing down goals is helpful and powerful. At the beginning of each day, write down the two things you decide to accomplish that day. Later, you may want to move into other goals; some may take longer than a day to accomplish. But try to do two things each day.

At the end of the day, let yourself feel good about the two things you've done. Do not judge yourself on how well you've accomplished them, or how difficult or easy the tasks were, or how you felt while doing them. Simply feel good that you did two things, especially when you didn't want to do anything. KLM

Set daily goals in times of crisis. You may also want to maintain another list of goals—the things you would like to see happen in your life. Write down anything you want, ask God to bring about all that is in your best good, then let go. Forget about your list and get back to your day.

TEN EASY THINGS TO DO ON DIFFICULT DAYS
1. Hold a baby
2. Walk along the beach
3. Tell someone you love them
4. Listen to oldies
5. Visit the zoo
6. Rent your favorite video
7. Call your grandmother
8. Buy yourself a gift
9. Write a story
10. Play with a dog

CCD

Pick a measurable, manageable task.

✳ Throughout our school years, we take tests. It consequently becomes easy to think of life as a series of tests, each with its pressure to get a good grade. One young woman was constantly grading herself in each task and situation. Finally she realized, "I think of my life as a pass/fail exam, with *pass* equal to 100 percent correct."

Do you get down on yourself for not accomplishing everything you set out to do in a day or a weekend? And does it all have to be perfect to be considered worth doing? Does the adage "Anything worth doing is worth doing right" have particular power over your thoughts?

Give yourself the freedom to enjoy a task. Start by picking one manageable task that can be easily tackled in an evening or a weekend. Perhaps it would feel good to get a set of errands out of the way. Or maybe there's an interesting repair or other household project that you can dig into and finish in the time you set aside. Maybe you've always wanted to build something, be it a model car or a birdhouse or a table, and you've shied away from it because you're sure "it wouldn't come out right." Don't worry about the results—the excess glue, the rough edges, the wobbly legs. Enjoy the task itself, and be proud of your initiative in trying it. Remember, anything worth doing . . . is simply worth doing. BRE

Pull out your calendar. Pick an evening or a weekend coming up soon to do one job that you can finish and enjoy doing. Ask for advice or help if necessary, but put away your grade book!

Take a fresh breath.

It was late at night. Depression was like white-hot pain in my soul.

"Breathe deeply," she intoned. She was my counselor—the only person I felt I could talk to that night. "Breathe in strength, and breathe out your pain! Breathe!"

It was good advice. Simple. Almost too simple. But I learned there's healing in a good fresh breath of life.

Doctors now prescribe deep breathing exercises for stress reduction. I know it works. Next time you feel under pressure—sitting in an airport, waiting for a business meeting to start, any tense moment—just take a deep, deep breath. Slowly fill your lungs and then release the air slowly. And again—ten times, slowly. You can just feel the stress go away, your stomach muscles loosen, and those short, nervous, jerky breaths become smooth again.

Try it on your depression.

Breathe in strength; breathe out weakness.

Breathe in courage; breathe out fear.

Breathe in health; breathe out pain.

Breathe in hope; breathe out sadness.

Often, when we are under duress, afraid, or in pain, we "stop" breathing. We may breathe shallowly or hold our breath for long periods of time. We get less oxygen, less life—when we need it most.

When you breathe deeply and deliberately, you are affirming life. You will feel calmer, more present, more alive. WW

Several times throughout the day, when you are busiest, most fearful, or most stressed, take two minutes to practice breathing.

Do something kind for someone you know.

✳ Someone once asked the great psychologist Karl Menninger, "What should a person do if he feels a nervous breakdown coming on?"

Menninger replied, "Lock the door of your house, go across the street, and do something to help your neighbor."

Sometimes doing something thoughtful for another person can ease our own pain. If we can forget our stress or heartache for even a moment, our head clears a bit. We come back to our own problems with a new perspective—at least enough to help us through another day.

Unfortunately, when we are particularly sad, we may suspect that nobody is as needy as we are or that we have nothing to give. *I'm in such darkness myself,* we may think. *How can I possibly help someone else?*

We also may be so conscious of the world's big problems that we forget the immediate opportunities to help out in the little things. Can stopping by to say hi to a lonely neighbor or taking a plate of cookies to a shut-in really make a difference?

More than we realize, the world is held together by the unpretentious deeds, the hidden acts of thoughtfulness. The poet Wordsworth spoke of the good done by the "little, nameless, unremembered acts of kindness and of love." Someone we know could use our simple offering of help, and we will feel better for having tried. TKJ

Think of someone you know who is having a hard time. Call, write a note, or go visit that person, thinking of some simple way to encourage him or her.

15 MOVIES TO WATCH

Call a friend or two, go to the video rental store, pick up some popcorn, and watch one of these movies:

1. E.T.
2. THE WIZARD OF OZ
3. THE SOUND OF MUSIC
4. IT'S A WONDERFUL LIFE
5. DRIVING MISS DAISY
6. ROCKY
7. CHARIOTS OF FIRE
8. MY LEFT FOOT
9. BABETTE'S FEAST
10. BRINGING UP BABY
11. BEN HUR
12. ORDINARY PEOPLE
13. TERMS OF ENDEARMENT
14. STEEL MAGNOLIAS
15. COCOON

Bake bread.

✳ "Love is sweet, but tastes better with bread"—an old Yiddish proverb.

There are at least two reasons why bread baking can give you a new lease on life:

1. It feels good to create something useful.
2. The bread smells so good.

These are the days of prebaked, prepreserved, presliced, pre-packaged bread. We have squeezed all the delight out of this richly historical food.

Bread started happening in the ancient world when the nomadic peoples finally settled down and grew grain. Egyptians skimmed the foam from fermenting wine and used it to make their bread rise. On the eve of their famous Exodus, the Israelites couldn't wait that long—and ever since, the "unleavened" bread of Passover has commemorated that miraculous escape.

Store-bought bread can't compete with the kind that people have been making themselves for thousands of years. Homemade bread is an investment of time and energy. You stretch a few sinews in kneading the dough. And it takes good timing to let it rise and punch it down at the right time. But it's worth it. The glorious smell of baking bread permeates the house. When bread is in the oven, we take nourishment with every breath.

A self-baked loaf is an achievement you can be proud of. And your family and friends will be grateful if you share it with them. RP

To learn how to bake bread, read Bernard Clayton's The New Complete Book of Breads *(Simon & Schuster) or* Laurel's Kitchen Bread Book *(Random House).*

Pray.

Sometimes, prayer is the last thing we feel like doing when we're depressed. What do we say to a God who seems as though he has disappeared? A God at whom we're angry—maybe rageful? A God we're not certain will hear, or answer us? Where do we find words to communicate our desperate need and confusion when we don't even understand it?

Some people use Scripture as prayers: Psalm 23 ("The Lord is my shepherd; I shall not want") or the Lord's Prayer, found in Luke 11:2-4 ("Our Father which art in heaven, hallowed be thy name") are helpful favorites.

Some people use excerpts from the *Big Book of Alcoholics Anonymous* as prayers: The Third Step prayer says: "God, I offer myself to thee . . . take away my difficulties, that victory over them may bear witness to those I would help" (page 63); or the Seventh Step prayer: "My Creator, I am now willing that you should have all of me, good and bad" (page 76).

Some religions have printed prayers available.

Some people look at the ceiling and just say, "Help."

Talk to God. Conscious, deliberate contact with God helps—even when we're not sure it will. LHJ

From the above suggestions, or your own ideas, write out a prayer that you like. Keep it taped to the mirror, where you can see it often. You might also want to go to a bookstore and purchase one of the many daily meditation books available. Choose one that appeals to you, or ask the clerk for assistance.

CHAPTER THREE

Alternatives That Take a Little Longer

*T*hese ideas suggest activities that take more than a moment, an hour, or a day. Many require a little more commitment than the "immediate alternatives," but that's good.

Committing to doing something helps us commit to being here, and that's what we're looking for: a commitment to being here with peace, even—especially—when we don't want to be here.

There's a suggestion in this section about getting a dog. Nichole and I got a puppy. Try it. Or get a cat. Or a hamster. Or a goldfish. Aquariums can contribute to a healing, peaceful environment. Not only do you have the little fish for pets, you have the relaxing benefits available from being able to look at water. Watch the intricate functioning of the underwater world. See the colors, the life, the movement, the harmony—the order and orderliness even with moments of chaos.

Some of the ideas in this section begin to suggest attitude changes: giving yourself time to heal; focusing on hope.

Many people find it helpful to surround themselves with positive, affirming messages. Some like to listen to meditation tapes—while they're cooking, driving the car, or lying in bed. Others like to read daily meditation books. There is an abundance of material available that will help support you in your decision to affirm life.

There are people who will help support you, too. Reach out to them. Let them reach out to you. Ask for help. Ask until you find it. Get involved with people, life, and living.

People do the darnedest things. They live longer than the doctors told them they would; and they decide to live fully until they die. A handicapped Irish author, Christopher Nolan, learned to peck words out on a keyboard with a pointer attached to his head. Jim Abbott, who lost a hand, is starting rotation pitcher for the California Angels.

Alcoholics get sober. Drug addicts do, too. People with codependency issues learn to love and care for themselves.

Teenagers—and adults—start over. They make new friends. They learn how to develop more meaningful relationships. People get out of debt. They find new jobs, develop new careers.

People learn how to fill their hours and days with meaningful activities.

They learn how to make peace with their lives.

Change is possible. But things take time.

Do some activities that require a little commitment while you're striving to make those changes.

Get a cat.

A cat can help you in many ways.
A kitten will make you laugh with its playful antics.

A cat will give you companionship, especially if you live alone. It will greet you at the door, ask politely for food, and watch intently while you sleep.

A cat will help you focus beyond yourself. By giving your cat the care it needs, you can have the satisfaction of doing something useful for someone else.

If you have love you want to give away, a cat will be happy to accept it. And if you feel like being alone, it will accommodate you.

If you take a kitten from a neighbor's accidental litter, you will make the neighbor happy. By swapping cat stories and ideas for cat care, you may make a new friend.

If you take a kitten or grown cat from the humane society, you are probably saving the cat's life. The cat will return the favor: pet owners are less likely to commit suicide than people without animals, and they are more likely to recover from serious illness.

Why get a cat? Practical reasons: cats are clean and quiet; they are often permitted by landlords who won't allow dogs; and they are warm and furry.

But cat lovers know that there is something about the grace, the stately beauty, the independence of a cat that goes far beyond the practical. HKN

Check the classified ads in the newspaper to see who's giving away kittens, or phone your local humane society.

Get a dog.

☀ No dog owner has to beg for love. A canine friend is always there to listen to you, no matter what you say. A wagging tail applauds any attention you give him. Dogs seem to know how to be happy along with you and, more important, they seem able to grieve with you when you hurt. They need you, and—like you— they need to feel needed. You never feel lonely with a dog at your feet—or on your lap.

Caring for dogs is easy. You can (1) make them sleep outside, (2) feed them the same food every meal for the rest of their life, and (3) bathe them only when they need it—like once a month! You don't have to do their laundry, send them to college, or fight with them over who gets the car.

Studies have shown that our heart rate and blood pressure drop when we pet dogs. Researchers have also found that cardiac patients with pets live longer than those without pets. In another study, senior citizens with dogs had fewer doctor visits over a one-year period than seniors without dogs. And experience has shown that the love you give a dog is returned a thousandfold. DJ

Contact your local SPCA or animal shelter for information on pet adoption. For a great source of pet information, write PAWS Prints, the newsletter of Pets are Wonderful Support, P. O. Box 460489, San Francisco, CA 94146-0489. Or call them at 415-824-4040.

Keep moving.

Even sharks know that the moment they quit moving they begin to sink to the bottom of the ocean.

Like sharks, when we stop moving, we're liable to start sinking. That's why it is important to keep ourselves occupied—with friends, work, or hobbies.

There are times when we need to slow down. But that doesn't mean we stop. For some, retirement means putting on the brakes. But people who choose only the rocking chair soon sink into depression. Eventually, like the motionless shark, they hit bottom.

The poet Tennyson gave a different picture of the elderly in his poem about the warrior-king Ulysses:

> *How dull it is to pause, to make an end,*
> *To rust unburnished, not to shine in use!*

Certainly, old age has its impairments. Yet, as Ulysses put it:

> *Though much is taken, much abides; and though*
> *We are not now that strength which in old days*
> *Moved earth and heaven, that which we are, we are—*
> *One equal temper of heroic hearts,*
> *Made weak by time and fate, but strong in will*
> *To strive, to seek, to find, and not to yield.*

Whatever your age, don't stop living. LW

If you can get out and around, volunteer to deliver Meals on Wheels. If you are restricted, visit a senior citizens' center and join with others in a hobby or discussion group. Look under Senior Citizens' Service Organizations *in the yellow pages or under your county government offices in the white pages of your phone book.*

Spend a morning with a child.

✳ Many of us could benefit by spending time with a little person. Yes, children are demanding, and at times exasperating. They honestly say what they need. They laugh and giggle when they're happy. They cry when they're hurt. They take naps when they're tired. They say no a lot, like to play, at times are self-indulgent, but love to give and receive hugs and kisses.

Their innocence is refreshing and renewing.

Morning activities are a good way to begin, since you avoid pre- and postnap crabbiness. Don't overstructure your time together, but do have a few things in mind. Older children may have favorite activities to propose; or try going out for breakfast, taking a camera with you to a playground, cruising a shopping mall, visiting a video store, or having a kiddie film fest in your home. If you're new to spending time with children, first get acquainted when they are with their parents. Spend time with them in their own homes, or invite the whole family over for a meal. Give each other time to warm up.

As you make friends in the under-four-feet-tall set, the joy and acceptance they offer may help you make friends with the child in you. John Greenleaf Whittier put it this way:

> We need love's tender lessons taught
> As only weakness can;
> God hath His small interpreters;
> The child must teach the man.

BRE

This week, start to develop a friendship with a child. Welcome children into your heart and home. Buy a few plastic cups for little guests and practice being calm when drinks are spilled.

Gather hugs.

Scotty taught me how to hug. His arms wrapped around my frightened body and pulled me close until I could feel his soothing strength reach to my very soul. His hug melted away some of the excruciating pain of divorce. He taught me that a hug could be nonsexual, with an incredible power to heal.

But Scotty was a busy man and could not always be available when I needed a hug. If I went more than a week without a hug, I found myself falling back into the tar pits of divorce depression. I soon realized that without hugs, the inner part of me might wither up and die.

I began to ask friends, both male and female, if I could get one hug a week from them. When appropriate, I asked the women for permission to be hugged by their spouse. I asked only those people who seemed to be affectionate in nature and secure in their marriage.

From that week on, it seemed my healing began a distinct progress. I had more strength to face the week. Soon I could believe I had value as a human being. For the hugs told me that I was loved, no matter what was happening to me or what mistakes I had made.

Studies of monkeys and babies have verified our need for human touch to survive, to thrive, to be happy and secure. Leo Buscaglia reaffirms this by saying, "A simple caress has the potential of changing a whole life." LHJ

Gather hugs from those who care. Try to get at least one hug a day and to give at least one hug a day.

Play.

✳ The playground is alive with sound: The ring of metal against the supporting pole ... The clank of chain as the tetherball flies, a golden globe of energy ... Children's shouts reverberating against the brick buildings ... Swings creaking in rhythm ... Sneakers thumping on asphalt.

What did you like to play when you were a small child? Did you jump rope? Blow bubbles? Create with clay? Slide? Maybe your play leaned more toward board games such as Monopoly or Sorry! or Life. Find that little child you knew so many years ago, that child who felt free to be silly, impulsive, creative, and imaginative.

Recapturing your childhood by playing can relieve stress in many ways. Active play relieves stress through cardiovascular exercise. All play shifts your mind from the struggles and depression that dominate it. As you play, you find your body relaxing, the tension in your muscles lessening. Bernie S. Siegel, M.D., author of *Love, Medicine and Miracles*, says, "Physiologists have found that muscle relaxation and anxiety cannot exist together." LHJ

List the things you enjoyed playing as a child. Then choose one activity to play for at least one hour. Borrow a small child to take to the park and slide with. Make play dough from scratch. Find a friend to play a board game with. Fly a kite. Roll down a grassy hill. Run. Skip. Play.

Travel to a place you've never been.

Your brain needs new experiences. It's a biological fact. "When the brain confronts the familiar—like the route you take to work every day—it tunes out and quiets down," writes psychologist Daniel Goleman in *American Health* (April 1988). "When you stay in the same place and do, more or less, the same things day after day, month after month, your brain becomes understimulated. Fortunately, the brain seems to have a built-in need to turn itself on—to explore, to seek out the novel."

That may explain why one study found that frequent travelers "worry less, feel less inhibited and submissive, and are more self-confident than stay-at-homes. They seem less neurotic" (Frank Farley, University of Wisconsin).

Scientists have traced this difference to a chemical in the brain, norepinephrine. Some people need this chemical more than others—these are the thrill seekers. But all of us need our brains tickled at least a little.

Some suicides are planned as "escapes." A person is sick and tired of his present life and wants to "get away from it all." Why not try hopping a plane first?

If plane fare is too steep for you, drive or take the bus and explore a new corner of your state. Picnic in a new park, or eat at an out-of-the-way diner. Your surroundings don't need to be posh, just different. Drink in these new experiences. Let that norepinephrine bubble up in your brain. RP

Contact a travel agent to find vacation plans within your budget. The agent may also have suggestions for local day trips. Or check travel books out of the public library.

Exercise.

✳ Jerry pulled the pillow over his head and slipped back into a deep sleep. He argued with everyone that he wasn't depressed, just tired. As soon as he caught up with his sleep, he would be fine.

Sleep became Jerry's drug, his escape from the fact that his wife of twenty years had left him. He no longer cared about his appearance, his work, his life. He missed his children, who had moved three hundred miles away. As far as Jerry was concerned, if his marriage died, he might as well die too.

Jerry's friend Mark began to goad him. He pestered him three times a week to get up early and just walk. They didn't walk far, or long. Soon Jerry was up and ready to go when Mark arrived. Eventually they began to jog.

Jerry's outlook on life became more positive. During the exercise, his mind cleared, and he began to see options for his future, for seeing his children, for dealing with his loss. He set small goals and obtained them.

Exercise relieves stress and alleviates depression. Tim Hansel says in *You Gotta Keep Dancin'*, "Exercise, especially of large muscle groups, produces chemicals that fight depression and low spirits. Believe it or not, exercise may be one of the most important things that we can do in the midst of pain or sorrow or grief. Walking, cycling, jogging or other aerobic exercise changes not only the chemicals in our bodies but our very attitudes." LHJ

Find an exercise you like and do it three times a week. Begin with ten minutes each time, working your way up to thirty or forty minutes. Walk the dog, jog, dance (it's difficult to stay depressed while dancing!), lift weights. Take a physical education class at a community college and make new friends while you're exercising.

Dig in the dirt.

☀ There is something about grubbing around in the dirt that revives the spirit. I'm not sure what makes it so therapeutic; it must arouse some primitive instinct. In today's world, gardening is the socially acceptable way to play in the mud.

For someone housebound, gardening may mean tending an African violet on the window sill. An apartment dweller may be limited to growing thyme and basil in balcony pots. But if at all possible, dig up a corner of your backyard, or reserve a plot in the community gardens.

My grandparents have grown a huge garden every summer for more than fifty years. So when I decided to plant my own, I wrote to them and enclosed a cassette tape. "Tell me all your gardening secrets," I said. The returned package included an Earl May catalog marked with their favorite hybrids. On the tape was their dinnertime conversation about the best burpless cucumbers and how to stake tomatoes so they don't rot on the ground. I treasure this tape, especially since my grandmother's death last year.

If you have no experience with gardening, seek out an expert. You can tell the experts by taking a walk around your neighborhood: the man whose rose bushes are painstakingly cared for, the woman who spends every spare moment in her strawberry beds. Gardeners love to talk about their hobby; just ask. You may gain a friend in the exchange. MSG

Call a nearby gardening center and ask for the addresses or phone numbers of several seed companies. Send for their catalogs, even if it's winter. You can sit by the fire and plan your garden, drooling over the prospect of a tasty harvest. By spring you'll be ready to grub in the dirt.

Watch killer whales.

Beautiful. Playful. Mysterious. *Big!* Killer whales (or orcas) are among the largest mammals on earth. Since they spend most of their life under ocean waves, most people don't see them. Whales are social animals and travel in pods of up to fifty whales. They live in the same pod for their entire life. Cooperation is important. Sometimes they will corral fish to eat. They play with one another—jumping into the air, flashing their white belly, splashing their tail.

To see whales, find an area where they're known to come. Then sit, either on land or in a boat, and wait until they appear.

Suddenly, without warning, a six-foot-high black triangle rises out of the ocean. That's the dorsal fin—a small part of the whale's body. Glistening. Graceful. Rhythmic. Another and then another. They come up for air, then go down to feed. They find nourishment in both the depths and heights, light and darkness of their world.

These ten-ton creatures can make you feel very small. But just being in their presence is a soul-expanding experience. They make you realize that even the largest and most mighty creatures help one another, work together to survive, and play together with abandon. DJ

Call your local aquarium for information on whales and whale watching. Or visit your library and check out books on orcas such as Orca, the Whale Called Killer *by E. Hoyt (Camden House Publishers) or* Killer Whales *by Bigg, Ellis, Ford, and Balcomb (Phantom Press and Publishers).*

Try wilderness therapy.

Nature has a way of giving us a new perspective. Ocean waves crashing on a deserted beach, a waterfall cascading down bare rock, the pink and orange of a desert sunset, clouds mirrored in a cold blue lake—these have a way of breathing life into our weary souls.

National and state parks offer opportunities to venture into nature without getting too far from home. Organizations like Summit Adventures and Outward Bound lead guided wilderness experiences even for the uninitiated. Retreat centers combine a beautiful setting with scheduled programs to nourish body, mind, and spirit.

Today there are treatment centers that incorporate treatment for addictions, psychological conditions, and depression with a wilderness experience. These treatment programs, which may be covered by insurance, combine traditional therapy with wilderness therapy. The great outdoors allows participants to experience real-life consequences, learn leadership skills, ask for help when it's needed, learn about powerlessness while building a support network, practice living in the present, and overcome obstacles.

A wilderness experience can give people more confidence in their ability to conquer other obstacles in life that previously seemed insurmountable. CN

Want to find out more about wilderness therapy? Phone one of these organizations:

* Summit Adventures 1-800-827-1282
* Outward Bound 1-800-882-8923
* National Outdoor Leadership School (Wyoming) 307-332-6973
* New Life Treatment Center Adolescent Wilderness Program 1-800-332-TEEN
* Christian Camping International (Illinois) 708-462-0300
* Association for Experiential Education (Colorado) 303-492-1547

Grow African violets ... and then give them away.

✳ Years ago it was discovered that elderly people living in nursing homes remained happier and healthier if they had living, growing plants to work with. The discovery even developed into a new field called horticultural therapy.

The well-known psychotherapist Milton Erickson tells of a woman who had suffered for many years with severe depression. Doctors had prescribed drugs and analysis, but nothing had worked. The woman lived under a constant dark cloud, isolated from human contact. Erickson decided to visit this woman in her home.

The first thing he noticed there was the flowers. Practically every table and surface was covered with African violets. The woman explained that growing flowers was the only thing in life that gave her pleasure. In the course of their conversation, she also mentioned a church she had attended in the past.

At the end of his visit, Erickson gave her his prescription: "I want you to grow African violets and give them to the people who attend that church you mentioned."

Months later, Erickson heard that the woman's depression had miraculously lifted. So many people were stopping by to see "the African violet lady" that she hardly had a moment to herself!

Not all depression can be cured that easily, but the story illustrates one antidote to chronic unhappiness. Do something you love, but don't stop there. Share what you love with others. You'll be nurturing not only your own spirit but also theirs. Best of all, you will no longer be alone. KM

Today, go to a plant nursery and choose a plant that appeals to you. Ask for instructions on how to help it thrive. Take it home and give it a place of honor. Maybe even name it and introduce it to a friend.

Let a book comfort or inspire you.

A panel of writers and booksellers met at the 1990 American Booksellers Association Convention in Las Vegas, Nevada, to discuss an important genre of books in American literature: recovery books. One panel member astutely mentioned that recovery books were books from all types of literature that help change, comfort, or inspire people.

A novel, a book of essays, a biography, a how-to-overcome book, a childhood favorite, or a meditation book can bring comfort, inspiration, and hope in times of need.

"There's something about reading, about immersing myself in another's world, where I can see how another person deals with overwhelming problems, that breaks the chain of my negative thoughts when I don't have the energy to stop them," said Marian.

Anne Morrow Lindbergh's classic *Gift from the Sea* is profoundly simple, easy to read, and inspirational. *Anne Frank: The Diary of a Young Girl* is described as a "song to life, no matter what the conditions, no matter what the threats."

Many have laughed, and been comforted, by Robert Fulghum's *All I Really Need to Know I Learned in Kindergarten.*

Many have learned they were not alone in their struggle to unwind the tangles of alcoholic families and find forgiveness for their parents by reading Louie Anderson's *Dear Dad: Letters from an Adult Child.*

Books on tape and large-print editions are bringing much of this literature to people who dislike or have difficulty reading.

Read a life-changing book today. Or reread your favorite one. KLM/CGP

Reread your favorite comforting or inspirational book. Or ask your librarian to help you find an inspirational biography. Keep a list of the most helpful books by your bed to remind you of their messages.

Make the psalms your own prayers.

In conversations with a hundred people of different faiths and denominations, including no religious affiliation, the Bible—and particularly the psalms—consistently emerged as favorite reading material that brought comfort in times of personal defeat and struggle.

"There is nothing new under the sun," wrote the writer of Ecclesiastes. Many of the psalms show that not much has changed about the human heart. Like people thousands of years ago, we still struggle with enemies within and without, we call out for help, we long to see God work faster, we wonder if we've been abandoned. Let these psalms express your doubts and fears.

Read them aloud or silently. Read through several until you find one that matches your circumstance or feelings.

Take a look at a few of the prayerlike variety. Psalm 3 expresses David's anguish as he flees from his son Absalom. Not only does he feel desperate, but people mock him. He is honest with God, who then answers him with sustaining sleep and deliverance.

Psalm 6 is written by one "weary with my moaning; every night I flood my bed with tears." Gradually the writer comes to trust that God has heard his weeping.

Psalm 73 presents a common question: How come the bad guys are doing so well and I'm in so much pain?

Psalm 103 is more upbeat, although the writer's heartaches show through.

The psalms have brought comfort and calm to many. They also show God's action in response to troubled people. Try using them to express yourself and to listen to God. BRE/LHJ

The psalms are easy to find. They are almost directly in the middle of the Bible. Try reading them, underlining God's action in response to pleas for help, and underlining the writer's emotions that parallel yours.

Underline everything in the Bible that makes you feel better.

Do you need reviving? Do you need joy? Try reading the Bible. Don't just read it. Chew on it. Mull it over. Find the things that help you. Underline these for future reference, and write notes to yourself in the margins. Some people don't like the idea of writing in the Bible. It's a holy book, they say, not to be defaced. Perhaps it's a family heirloom with a leather cover and see-through pages. By all means spare that Bible. Go to any bookstore and buy an inexpensive paperback Bible in a modern, easy-to-understand translation. Get a ballpoint pen or a highlighter, and start under-lining.

Don't start at the beginning. You'll get hung up somewhere in Leviticus. Start with the psalms. Then read John, Acts, and Romans, or the second half of Isaiah. Underline sentences and phrases you find especially helpful. Come back to these later when you're feeling down. You may be surprised that not everything you read there is "inspirational." The psalms contain a lot more than "The Lord is my shepherd." David often complains about how unfair life is.

U.S. President Woodrow Wilson once spoke of the Bible in this way: "A man has found himself when he has found his relation-ship to the rest of the universe, and here is the Book in which those relations are set forth." RP

The easiest Bible versions to understand are The Living Bible *and* Today's English Version. *Other popular modern versions include the* New Revised Standard Version, *the* New International Version, *and the* New Jerusalem Bible. *The King James (or Authorized) Version contains the traditional wording but may be hard to understand unless you're a Shakespeare buff.*

Remember a time when life was simpler.

✳ The day my friend Martha died, I got on my daughter's swing and swung for two hours.

That day I realized that rocking, or swinging, is a movement that speaks comfortingly to a hidden part of me. It's a memory that comes from infancy when I was comforted with rocking in my mother's arms. Along with the memory of rocking comes the recollection of my mother stroking the lashes of my closed eyelids.

Most of us have a few sensations that remind us of better, simpler, more childlike times. Perhaps it is the smell of popcorn on the stove or the crackle of a fire. Perhaps it is a piece of music or an old TV show. Perhaps being wrapped closely in fluffy blankets makes us feel secure. Maybe we respond to the smell of baking bread or a roasting turkey. Maybe it's the taste of peppermint and the twinkle of Christmas lights in the dark that remind us of a time when play was our way of life.

If we can find again those fleeting moments of security and pleasure, perhaps we can find a way to soothe ourselves when life has overtaken us and playfulness seems a thousand miles away. JG

Do something today that you haven't done in a long time—something that reminds you of special times and warm feelings. Take time to savor the feelings it stirs up.

Join a theater group.

There's nothing quite as exciting as an opening night, whether on Broadway or at your local community theater. The play has been practiced, the sets built, the lights hung, the costumes sewn, the programs printed; and now the ushers stand in place to greet the crowd.

But the thrill of opening night is just the outside of a rich inner experience—the joy of bringing something to life. Think of it. A play starts as words on paper and a vision in a director's mind. Six weeks later it's an event. That's what people celebrate on opening night—the miracle of birth. There are many ways in which you can be part of the experience.

Acting. Acting broadens a person by introducing him to different situations, different emotions. Most actors get to know themselves better in the process. You probably won't step into a lead role right away, but supporting parts can be just as satisfying. And maybe, after some acting classes and chorus parts, who knows?

Technical help. Most amateur theaters need all the behind-the-scenes help they can get. Do you know electronics? Maybe you can work with the light or sound equipment. Can you build things or sew? Sets and costumes are needed for most shows.

Support staff. Many theaters need ushers or concessions workers or typists or people to paste labels on their flyers. This isn't glamorous work, but it's part of the process. And you'll meet a lot of interesting people doing it. RP

Look in the newspaper for amateur productions in your area. Contact the theater and volunteer your services. Or start attending performances in your area, and support theater by your presence at opening night.

Volunteer to help others.

Loneliness. Isolation. Alienation. Feelings of uselessness and low self-esteem. These all contribute to a person's suicidal inclinations.

Giving your time and energy to help someone else can alleviate these feelings. For some people, it gives them a reason to go on living.

Helping others makes us happy. It may also make us healthy. Research reported by Catherine Houck in *Woman's Day* "found that doing regular volunteer work, more than any other activity, dramatically increased life expectancy. Men who did no volunteer work were two and a half times as likely to die during the study as those who donated time at least once a week."

The article concluded, "To enjoy health benefits from volunteer work, you must do it on a regular basis."

Volunteering gives you concrete evidence of your own value. It gives you the opportunity to use and develop your skills, and it puts you in contact with many people who may become friends. It gets you out of the house into the world of activity, and it focuses your attention outside yourself.

Obviously, volunteer work cannot substitute for getting appropriate medical or psychological care or for volunteering to take care of yourself. Something in your life drove you to thoughts of suicide, and you must pay attention to what it was. But once the crisis is over—and even while you are getting help for it—volunteering can keep you in touch with people who need you. That can be a tremendous incentive to go on living. CN

Your local chamber of commerce will be able to direct you to organizations in your area that use volunteers. Also check with churches, schools, and civic organizations to find out their needs.

A SAMPLING OF ORGANIZATIONS THAT NEED VOLUNTEERS

Big Brothers and Big Sisters (Pennsylvania) 215-567-7000
Catholic Charities (DC) 202-639-8400
Foster Parents/Grandparents Program—check your phone book
Habitat for Humanity (Georgia) 912-924-6935
Literacy Volunteers of America (New York) 315-445-8000
Meals on Wheels—check your phone book
National AIDS Network (DC) 202-293-2437
National Coalition Against Child Abuse (Illinois) 312-663-3520
National Coalition for the Homeless (DC) 202-659-3310
Recording for the Blind (New Jersey) 609-452-0606
United Way (Virginia) 703-836-7100
Volunteers in Service to America (VISTA, the domestic Peace Corps) (DC) 202-634-9445

These suggestions only scratch the surface. To learn about needs in your community, check the library, your church, or the newspaper for volunteering opportunities. Also check your phone book to see if these organizations have local numbers. Phone a group that interests you and see if your skills match their needs.

Go on a personal treasure hunt.

Have you ever known someone who just can't take a compliment?

"You look nice today."

"No, I don't."

"You're fun to be with."

"No, I talk too much."

For every positive thing you say, this person comes back with two negatives.

Self-esteem, or the lack of it, is a major problem for many. Mark Twain said it succinctly: "A man cannot be comfortable without his own approval."

Maybe you're in that boat.

Here's a project for you. Compile a list of ten good things about you. Where do you get these things? From other people—you can't make them up yourself.

1. Start by listing twelve friends, relatives, or acquaintances you can contact to do your research (ten plus two alternates in case some don't take you seriously). These could include everyone from your spouse to the cashier at 7-Eleven.

2. Contact these people and say something like this: "I'm doing a research project [you are!] and I need you to tell me one good thing about me." If they say something that's already on the list, ask them for something else.

3. Make up your "Top Ten" list and post it where you'll see it every day.

4. Make a point of saying something nice to all the people you contacted. RP

It is difficult to make a man miserable while he feels worthy of himself and claims kindred to the God who made him. ◆ Abraham Lincoln

Tell one hundred people how you feel.

✳ Communication can be a problem. No one seems to care. No one understands. No one can do anything about your needs. You feel awful, depressed, and all alone.

So tell someone about it.

Don't just tell one person. Your problems deserve a greater audience. Tell a hundred. That may take some effort. How many people do you normally talk to in a day? Ten? Twenty? It may take some time and planning to reach a hundred. But make it a project.

Most suicides are primarily attempts to communicate. Psychologist Edwin Shneidman writes, "It is a sad fact that suicides are not essentially acts of hostility or revenge, but are individuals' attempts to get others to see their pain" (*Psychology Today*, March 1987).

What will happen with your hundred listeners? Well, some won't really listen. Count on that. Others will listen and not take you seriously. Others will be so wrapped up in their own problems, they won't care about yours.

But two things will happen. (1) Some will care. And they may do things to help. They will at least provide a sympathetic ear. (2) Someone is bound to start telling you about his problems, and you may begin to care about that person. Either way, it's a lifeline for you. RP

Get some pages of lined paper and write the numbers 1 to 100. Start by listing all the people you expect to see in the next few days. Check their names off as you tell them your problems. Fill in the names of others as you tell them. If you find it hard to talk about your difficulties, say, "I'm doing this project I read about in a book. Listen to me for sixty seconds, okay?"

Share your pain with others who care.

✳ No words have been invented in the English language that are able to describe the dark, cold, foggy pit of despair I moved in daily. Life seemed to offer only eternal pain. I had a gun that offered eternal rest.

In my desperate search for a way out, I often contemplated the ticket to freedom resting on the closet shelf.

One night I made the final choice to stop the pain forever.

I had decided to first call a new friend who had seemed to understand and care about the intense pain that smothered me. He lived two states away. But the distance didn't stop him and his wife from pouring out their offerings of hugs, love, acceptance, and support. They wanted me alive.

I hung up the phone, unable to control the shaking in my whole being. I sat on my hands, afraid if I didn't, they would reach for the gun against my new wishes. If these people loved me, then there *must* be a reason to live, to go on. If they loved me, perhaps others did, too. I began to list them, and discovered more than I imagined. Each of those people valued my presence, my contribution to their lives.

I gingerly began to share my pain with others on my list. Their love gave me the support I needed to continue living. In turn, some shared with me their own journey through pain and depression. I discovered how they healed and survived and that I could too. LHJ

Call a friend now. If you can't reach the friend, call a suicide hotline. Look in the yellow pages under Community Services *or* Counseling, *or in the white pages under* Suicide. *If you don't find a hotline, call the Suicide Prevention Hotline at 1-800-333-4444.*

Keep a journal of your thoughts and feelings.

Writers keep journals to hone their craft. Public figures keep journals for posterity. The brilliant Civil War epic on PBS drew largely from the journals of common people. And millions of pre-teen girls still record their passions and crushes in secret diaries.

Now comes experimental evidence that writing can keep you healthy. A group of students at Southern Methodist University was asked to spend fifteen minutes a day for four days writing about traumatic experiences they had faced.

Did they feel better afterward? Not right away. But four months later, their moods were greatly improved. "Writing about their deepest thoughts had started a process that resulted in a lighter mood and more positive outlook," wrote researcher James W. Pennebaker (*American Health*, Jan/Feb 1991). And in the six months after the writing, they had had fewer health problems than before.

Researchers tested the immune cells in the blood of the journal writers before and after the experiment. "The findings were unequivocal," says Pennebaker. "People who wrote thoughtfully and emotionally about traumatic experiences showed heightened immune function compared with those who wrote about superficial topics."

Writing changed not only their psychology, but their biology. One student said, "I was finally able to deal with it and work through the pain instead of trying to block it out. Now it doesn't hurt to think about it." RP

Get a blank notebook and write fifteen minutes a day. Don't start with your biggest trauma. Just write what you're feeling and why. You'll get to the big stuff. Keep your journal to yourself. And don't be surprised if you feel a bit melancholy after writing. That feeling will go away soon.

Write your memoirs.

My grandmother is ninety-five years old. I talked with her as we heard news reports of the forces gathering for Desert Storm. "What was it like in World War I?" I asked her (she was a teenager when that war started). "Were you in favor of the U.S. getting involved?"

She has answered many questions like that over the years. "How was it for you in the Depression?" "What did you think of FDR?" "How did you feel when you got the right to vote?" The crazy events of our modern world take on a new perspective through her eyes. Surprised by the demise of communism in Russia? She remembers when they had a czar.

I will miss her when she's gone. I have asked her to write down as much as she can remember about her growing-up years. And she has written delightfully about the one-room schoolhouse, the farm chores, the sleigh ride to church on snowy Sunday mornings.

What stories can you tell? Even if you're still young, you have a unique life experience to share. Your views of your world, your time, your people, can give great perspective to those around you.

Your memories are needed. They're valuable to you and others. The world has hurtled through massive changes in this century. Maybe you have, too. Write about them. RP

A simple way to write memoirs is a writing exercise developed by Natalie Goldberg, author of Writing Down the Bones *and* Wild Mind. *Get a notebook, start with "I remember" and write for ten minutes, nonstop. Whenever you pause, force yourself to return to "I remember." Then, spend ten minutes writing about "I don't remember." You may be surprised at what you do and don't recall.*

Plan the hard days ahead of time.

✳ Those who have suffered a major loss know that some days are harder than others. The hardest are anniversaries and holidays.

One year had passed since Rolie and Mike lost their four-year-old son Kyle to a sudden illness. Their grief penetrated deeply. When I called them on that first anniversary, Rolie told me, "We've decided to go to a concert by the group *Glad*. Their version of 'A Mighty Fortress' was Kyle's favorite song. We felt it would be a fitting way to remember his life." Though they knew tears would flow freely during the concert, Rolie and Mike sensed the importance of making plans for that difficult day.

After my fiancé died, I knew I could not bear to sit alone and cry on the upcoming anniversary of our engagement. So I enlisted several friends to enter a five-mile run/walk which would raise money for the local diabetes association. As I walked that course, the crunch of leaves underfoot and the crisp fall air reminded me of our engagement day. But by participating in the event, I was surrounded by friends who cared about me, and I was helping a cause I believed in. It made the day more bearable.

It is important to have time alone to reflect and cry. But for most people who have suffered a loss, those times are plentiful. Plan ahead to be with people and in places that can help you make it through these anniversaries and holidays. MSG

Take out a calendar and circle in red the dates you know will be especially hard for you. Check your local newspaper for upcoming events, or think about an activity you would enjoy. Enlist your friends or family to help you make plans for these days. Then follow through.

Take yourself seriously—but not too seriously.

✳ The ability to get through the worst days often boils down to knowing what to look at with resolve and what to look at with humor.

First, take yourself seriously. Know that you and your problems are worth dealing with. Your health is worth seeking medical attention. The depression you suffer and the hurt you feel are real. You are unique and so is your situation; do what you must to regain your health. There may be those around you who minimize your problems. Don't listen to their flip remarks.

And yet, don't take yourself too seriously. Hold on to your sense of humor. It is one of life's most precious gifts and will get you through the most painful days. Let yourself laugh, even if only to yourself, for laughter will buy you some time—another of life's gifts.

One evening, four people were gathered in a room. One woman had recently attended the funerals of her father and best friend. Another woman had just buried her son. A teenage girl, a victim of sexual abuse, had lost her father to alcoholism and her only brother in an accident. Another teenage girl had experienced a pregnancy, recently buried her grandfather, and learned her other grandfather was terminally ill.

This question was asked of each of them: "Are there any situations in life too grim to be brightened by a sense of humor?"

Each answered, immediately, "No!"

Regardless of your situation, it's OK to maintain a sense of humor. In fact, it may be necessary. BRE

Read a good book on taking yourself and life seriously. One recommendation: The Road Less Traveled *by M. Scott Peck, M.D. Then find comic relief: spend time with a friend who has a sense of humor.*

Make yourself as comfortable as possible.

Laura lay in the darkened room. Her heart physically ached; her emotional pain was dull, thick, and black. Her husband had been killed in an automobile accident some years ago. Now, her boyfriend had just ended their engagement.

The phone rang. It was a friend from another city. He knew her well—he knew how she handled pain, and he often intuitively sensed when she was in it.

"How are you?" he asked.

"Not good," she said.

"I know," he replied. "But why don't you stop punishing yourself? Pop some popcorn, turn on the television, snuggle up with the kids under a comforter, and be good to yourself. You hurt enough," he said. "Don't make it worse by punishing yourself."

Many of us are in severe pain—emotional or physical. It hurts. To deny that is absurd. Suffering and pain that can't be avoided can't be avoided. Not all physical pain can be relieved by medication. The shock and grief of losing a loved one or finding out that you have a terminal illness hurts. Bankruptcy hurts. Relationship problems hurt.

But we don't have to make ourselves feel worse when we already feel bad enough.

We can let people in, instead of pushing them away. We can take medications that help relieve as much physical pain as possible. We can talk to someone on the phone. Watch a baseball game. Play music we enjoy. Talk to God. Paint our fingernails . . .

We can find ways to make ourselves as comfortable as possible while we're going through legitimate pain and suffering. KLM

Look around. What are the little—or big—things you could do right now to make yourself more comfortable? Often, a little relief is a decision and an action away.

A special message for teens: Listen to your life.

Life isn't simple anymore. On the one hand, that's good. Computers can process information as quickly as a heartbeat. Scientists can find cures for terrible diseases.

On the other hand, that's not so good. Sometimes, in the whirlwind of everyday pressures at school and at home, you begin to feel worthless . . . lost. You wonder, *Who am I? Does anyone care? Am I worthwhile? Is life really worth living?*

Tough questions. They might even seem frightening. But don't let them scare you. You are stronger than your questions. Besides, you don't have to find answers right away. Rainer Maria Rilke, a poet, wrote to another young poet:

> You are so young, . . . and I want to beg you, as much as I can . . . to be patient toward all that is unsolved in your heart and try to love the *questions themselves* like locked rooms and like books that are written in a very foreign tongue. Do not now seek the answers, which cannot be given you because you would not be able to live them. . . . Live everything. *Live* the questions now.

What does that mean, "live your questions"? You may feel as though no one is listening to you. Why not try listening yourself? Listen to what is really going on inside. Maybe you'll need help from someone—your parents, your best friend, or a school counselor. But listen. Listen to your life.

Don't worry if you don't hear anything. That's OK. Take a deep breath and realize that *this doesn't mean you are empty inside.* You have a wonderful story inside. It's worth listening for; it's worth telling. You may want to write down what you hear. Or maybe you'll want to paint a picture, sing, or dance. Do it. Get it out and get it down. Even if it seems ugly and dark. It's still you. That makes it worthwhile.

You are special. Don't let anyone or anything convince you otherwise. Life deserves someone special like you. Don't let darkness—perhaps even death—carry you away. Let life carry you away instead. Let *you* carry you away. Live everything! Listen. You're worth it. SJA

If you need someone to listen to you, call the Suicide Prevention Hotline: 1-800-333-4444.

Allow time to heal.

In a society expecting instant food, instant cash, and instant answers, we often wonder what's wrong with us when we do not have instant healing or instant grief resolution. I've heard well-meaning consolers tell the mother of a dead child that "God must have needed that child more than you." Or say to a person freshly grieving a dissolved marriage, "Don't worry, there's plenty more fish in the sea."

We demand others to heal quickly, feeling it should take as much time to heal from a broken heart as it does to heal from a broken limb. When it is our turn to hurt, we demand the same instant healing from ourselves. Anything less is a weakness. And yet deep wounds require a long time to heal. Rushing the process does not heal the wound; it only hides it and makes it take even longer to heal.

Robert Veningao, in his book *A Gift of Hope*, encourages us to allow time to heal: "Human pain does not let go of its grip at one point in time. Rather, it works its way out of our consciousness over time. There is a season of sadness. A season of anger. A season of tranquillity. A season of hope." Allow yourself to pass through the seasons of healing just as you pass through the seasons of a year, knowing that winter will eventually end and spring will come. LHJ

Read A Gift of Hope *by Robert Veningao as reassurance that the healing will come in time.*

Live one day at a time.

Many of us spend our lives playing the "what if" game. What if I never get married again? What if this depression lasts ten more years? What if I lose my house? What if the pain gets worse? Our emotions rage: we are angry about the past, afraid for the future, and anxious about today. The spiral continues when we let today's anxiety lead us to more worry about tomorrow and the next day.

If we've spent too many years in that kind of cycle, there is a secret that we can learn. That secret is to live each and every moment.

Many recovery groups teach this principle. Someone addicted to a substance may not be able to fathom the idea of remaining clean and sober for the next thirty years. But can they survive another hour? Can they make it until bedtime? It's a lot easier to face a few hours than it is to face a lifetime.

How about you? Can you survive your emotional or physical pain until this evening? Why bother thinking about one year, one month, or even one week from now? You may not be able to change your current situation immediately, but you can change the way you think about it. When it seems you can't go on, ask yourself, *Can I make it through this day?* Or even, *Can I make it just one more second?* Before you even answer, you've succeeded. CCD

Today, practice living in the present moment. Feel what you feel now, not what you might feel tomorrow. Do what is on your agenda for today, and other than commonsense planning (which may be less planning than you believe), let tomorrow's activities dictate themselves.

CHAPTER FOUR

Alternatives That Bring Change

This is the big stuff here. Now that you've bought yourself a dog, get down on the floor and let yourself play with him instead of curling up your nose and wondering what he's going to chew.

If you have an underlying problem, like addiction or codependency issues, take action steps to solve that problem. Find a therapist. Go to treatment. Go to a support group.

Make friends. Get involved in relationships with *people*. Learn to love them, and let them love you. Maybe you've lost someone you love, someone that was a big part of your reason to live. Find other ways to express that love, and repair the hole in your heart.

"You don't see it yet," a friend said, "but you will, someday. You'll realize how lucky you were to have loved so intensely."

Learn to love yourself. Figure out what that means.

Find and nurture your passion—for living and healing.

If you have a physical ailment, go to a doctor and begin treating it.

If you have learned you have a terminal illness, take the steps you need to deal with that. Facing death, mortality, and the loss of our physical body is a tremendous challenge.

So is living fully until that happens.

I used to think that there was a "death age," kind of like the legal age for getting a driver's license. To my way of thinking, people lived until a certain time (somewhere in the late eighties), and then, when they reached that age, they died.

After Shane died, I started reading the obituaries. It wasn't any kind of morbid fascination or curiosity about *who* died. I read the ages because then I didn't feel like life had singled me out or was picking on me.

Some people die before they're born. Some shortly after. Some before the first year. Some at age seven.

Some at twelve.

Some in their twenties, thirties, forties—every age from zero to more than one hundred.

Some of us learn how much time we've got left. Others are left guessing. There is much grief and many other complex emotions involved with facing our death. But once we do, we can creatively make responsible choices concerning it, such as writing wills—including living wills—funeral arrangements, hospice and home care, and other important, relevant matters.

After we've done that, we can return to the matter at hand: living. We can figure out what we want to do with each day of our life and how to make each day count—for ourself, for those we love, for a higher purpose.

We can aggressively treat physical pain if our illness is terminal. We can finish up unfinished business, tie up loose ends, and say not just good-bye but also hello to those we care about.

Maybe you'll find a miracle of physical healing. Perhaps you'll encounter another kind of miracle and healing—one that does not eliminate the disease you're living with but instead cures the spirit.

Here is one more alternative I've found helpful, whatever the particular circumstances we're experiencing. This idea is also expressed in the excellent article titled "Find a Mentor" (page 114), but I want to say a little more here.

Get a buddy. Remember when we were young, how we went on the buddy system when we went through something scary or dangerous—like swimming at camp? We can go on the buddy system again. Find a partner, a friend, a buddy—someone who will commit to holding your hand and going through your experience, step-by-step, with you.

You are not burdening this person. You are giving him or her—and yourself—a gift.

When I got sober, I needed a buddy, someone to hold my hand and help me find my way through that confusing process.

When my children were born, I wanted someone to go through the experience with me—come into the labor room, coach me, hold my hand, watch me scream, then watch me cry with joy when I held my new baby. My husband (now my ex) didn't want to, so I got a buddy—a best friend—to do this with me.

When my son died, I needed to go back on the buddy system. My same friend, my buddy, who went into the delivery room with me when Shane was born, stood by my side in the hospital room the night he died.

She helped me find a mortuary. She went into the room with me—the one with the coffins in it—and stood by my side while I sat on the floor and cried. She stood quietly by while I yelled out, "What do you mean, which one do I prefer? Don't you understand I don't *prefer* any of them?" Then she held my hand, helped me get up, and helped me choose.

You don't have to do it alone. Your buddy probably won't be able to be there all the time. Sometimes he or she will need a break, or something else will come up. But let someone be there for you.

"I believe that pain and creativity are closely connected," my friend Dave, a minister, said one day. "And I don't just mean the kind of creativity we use to sculpt, draw, or write—although that's included."

He was talking about a deeper creativity—one that embraced creativity in loving, in giving, in healing—in relationship.

Let your pain ignite creativity in you.

Seek help for powerful or confusing emotions.

Late one evening, after Marty's counselor suggested that Marty "fully enter" her disappointment with life, Marty pictured herself draining the blood out of her body with a knife, and leaving her pain and despair behind. Only a fear of going to hell stopped her from acting it out, she said.

Two days later, Marty no longer felt suicidal. Her hopelessness didn't disappear instantly, but by the next evening, in the midst of bedtime stories, clean pajamas, and soft-skinned children, she noticed that the gut-wrenching waves of pain had left her.

Sometimes, in the process of "getting it all out," we come across emotions or experiences that are too powerful, bleak, and black for us to handle alone.

Sometimes, suicidal thoughts or attempts accompany the surfacing of repressed incidents of abuse.

If your feelings become too black, powerful, or out-of-control, get help. Tell someone. Investigate. See if there is an underlying problem symbolized by the suicidal thoughts such as sexual or physical abuse. Often, victims repress abuse incidents so thoroughly that they cannot consciously remember it happening. KLM

If you are feeling suicidal, call your therapist or an abuse hotline. If you suspect you're a victim of sexual abuse, seek out professional help, or a support group. Call Adcare Referral, 1-800-252-6465, to locate help in your area.

Get it all out.

Anger. Fear. Despair. Hopelessness. Feeling limited, rejected, alone. Betrayed. Overwhelming grief. Rage. Panic. Terror.

The list of feelings we experience is long. Sometimes we don't allow ourselves to feel. We hold our feelings inside, tucked away. They may start to come out, but we force them back. "Shouldn't feel that way. Don't want to feel that way. Afraid to feel that way." But denying feelings doesn't make them go away. It makes us tired, apathetic, sick, and stuck.

Often, beliefs are connected to feelings. We feel rageful because we believe God has abandoned us. We feel terrified because we believe we're unlovable. We feel limited because we believe we're doomed.

A common wisdom among professionals is that we need to get it all out—not deny our feelings and beliefs—in order to be free of them. We don't change by pretending.

This process sounds easy, but can be intense. And "getting it all out" doesn't mean hurting ourselves, or anyone else. It means we take responsibility for our feelings and beliefs as well as our process of healing them. If you begin the process, seek help from a therapist or counselor who will commit to guiding you through.

There are many options and sources of help available that can assist us in getting our old feelings and beliefs out. Therapists and support groups can help and encourage us. Keeping a journal, letter writing (these don't have to be sent), talking, crying, driving in the car screaming, can help. KLM

Develop a structured plan for getting out old and current emotions. This may include therapy, time with a friend, or time spent writing. Or all three. If a friend assists you, make certain this person knows what you're trying to accomplish, and is willing to listen and help.

Let yourself grieve.

If you've lost someone or something very dear, you know about well-meaning people who are quick to give advice. After my fiancé was killed in a violent explosion, I was occasionally the subject of platitudes and advice. But one suggestion ran counter to the Band-Aid solutions.

As the funeral guests gathered, my friend Hal told me of a loss he had suffered many years before. "I wasn't given permission to grieve," he said. "I felt I had to hold all my feelings inside. And so I am going to pray that you will allow yourself to grieve this loss fully."

Psychologists say that resolving acute grief can take two full years. It is pointless and damaging to try to railroad ourselves through the process.

For me, grieving meant
* wanting to scream out at God
* accepting that I did not enjoy life at that point
* letting myself consider suicide and reject the idea
* crying myself to sleep at night
* holding on to friends who were not threatened by my grief
* allowing the stages of grief—denial, anger, bargaining, depression, acceptance—to run their course

The process may be different for you, but one thing is sure—it will take time. So let yourself grieve. MSG/CN

Read a book on grief such as Dr. Elizabeth Kubler-Ross's On Death and Dying, *C. S. Lewis's* A Grief Observed, *or John W. James and Frank Cherry's* The Grief Recovery Handbook: A Step-by-Step Program for Moving Beyond Loss. *Share your grief with a counselor or a few close friends, and don't worry about explaining yourself to anyone else. Contact the Grief Recovery Institute (California) at 213-650-1234 for a referral to a grief therapist or support group.*

Find healing from sexual shame

Dear friend:

I might be your father. Your brother. Your uncle. The man you babysit for.

Maybe I'm your mother. Your sister. Your neighborhood teen-aged babysitter.

Or maybe I'm a counselor at your school. The leader of your Boy Scout group. A minister at your church.

The thing is, you trust me.

Sometimes when we're alone, I do things to you. I might show you my genitals. Or touch yours. I might have intercourse with you. Or do something else sexual. Then I tell you not to tell anyone. Ever. Because something bad will happen.

Because you trust me, because you're young and think I know what I'm doing, you feel ashamed. And scared.

I'm just writing this letter to let you know that you haven't done anything wrong, even if you didn't fight me off. It's my problem. I didn't want you to tell anyone because then I'll have to deal with my problem. And I'm so very ashamed.

The best thing you can do for both of us is tell someone. Now. Tell as many people as you need to, until someone listens, and cares, and helps you. And me.

Maybe you feel shame for something that was done to you. Maybe you feel guilty for sexual things you've done to someone else. Regardless of your age, if you're doing things you don't like *with* or *to* other people, or if someone is doing things to you, get help. You deserve it. CN

Healing from sexual shame and out-of-control sexual behaviors is possible at any age. Call 1-800-227-LIFE to talk to a counselor who can help you get started.

Find relief from guilt.

Seventeen and unmarried, Tina discovered she was pregnant. Brought up in a strict religious home, Tina thought it would kill her parents to find out. And she felt God would never forgive her. There was no way out, she thought. So she took her own life.

What Tina didn't realize was that her parents would rather have had a living pregnant daughter than a dead one. She also didn't realize that mercy and forgiveness are God's forté.

Shame, guilt, and fear of humiliation can, in times of duress, look more formidable than death.

They needn't be that powerful, nor formidable. We can find a way other than punishing ourselves to deal with guilt and shame.

Guilt over our behavior can be absolved. The Twelve Step programs offer a procedure for doing that: make a written moral inventory; admit our wrongs and faults to ourselves, God, and one other human being; make a list of the people we've harmed; become willing to have God remove these defects of character; become willing to then make direct amends to these people; then accept God's forgiveness and let guilt go. Forgive ourselves.

Most religions offer their own, specific formula for confessing and absolving guilt.

Recovery groups and some sound thinking can help us work through non-legitimate guilt (habitually feeling guilty because of what someone else has done, or feeling guilty when we haven't done anything wrong but others tell us we should feel guilty).

"We are going to know a new freedom and a new happiness. We will not regret the past nor wish to shut the door on it. We will comprehend the word serenity and we will know peace. No matter how far down the scale we have gone, we will see how our experience can benefit others" (Alcoholics Anonymous, *Big Book*). JKE/KLM

Read John Bradshaw's Healing the Shame That Binds Us.

Seek treatment for alcohol addiction.

A woman was found dead on the bathroom floor, an empty bottle of pills and an empty bottle of whiskey nearby. For one year, Barbara had won in her struggle against alcohol. Then she slipped, just for one night. She felt defeated—permanently.

Mark had been an alcoholic ever since he could remember. So were his brothers, their father, and their grandfather. Mark said he could quit but kept on drinking while his wife, children, job, and money slipped away.

Then one night Mark was arrested for drunk driving. When he woke up on the bottom bunk of the Saturday night drunk tank, he cried out in desperation to a God he didn't yet know. A few days later, Mark committed his life to Christ *and* joined Alcoholics Anonymous. For Mark, that was the first step. Today, more than ten years later, Mark—with God's help—has put his life back together again.

Many alcoholics are depressed, even if they do not realize it. People who bring their alcohol abuse under control significantly reduce their risk of suicide. They also reduce their risk of dying from other alcohol-related disorders.

If depression and alcohol abuse have been present in your life, seek inpatient alcoholism treatment in a medical facility that can monitor your depression as you break away from the alcohol dependency.

If you have gotten sober, then slipped, contact either a member of your Alcoholics Anonymous group or a treatment facility for help. CN/ERS

Adcare Referral is a 24-hour hotline in Worcester, Massachusetts, that can refer you to treatment facilities for alcohol, drugs, sex, gambling, or psychiatric problems. Adcare also can help you find an Alcoholics Anonymous, Al-Anon, or Codependents Anonymous group in your area. Call 1-800-252-6465.

Get help for struggles related to sexual orientation.

✳ Elizabeth, an attractive, articulate writer, was thirty-three years old and seldom dated, preferring close emotional relationships with women.

As a child and teenager, Elizabeth had been emotionally, physically, and sexually abused by *both* of her parents—so much so that she had spent most of her life living as though she had no physical body at all. In her thirties, she began to feel sensations that she had only felt when she was afraid as a child. She wanted to physically die; to kill that part of herself that could hurt her.

Elizabeth knew she couldn't spend the rest of her life pretending to have no body. She had been called, by God, to wholeness. She began to date men, but something seemed to be missing. "Am I a lesbian?" she asked God one morning.

Greg desperately wanted to be like the other guys, but he didn't fit in. A high-school teacher, trying to be helpful, told him that there was nothing wrong with being homosexual.

Greg was horrified. Already frightened by his emerging sexuality, he didn't want to consider the possibility that he was homosexual. "I'd rather be dead!" he shouted. For the first time, Greg became suicidal.

Sexual orientation issues are controversial and complex. But the complexities often cause the most pain and confusion within the person who is struggling through sexual orientation issues.

As a group, homosexuals have a higher-than-average suicide rate. The rate among homosexual teens is especially high.

The issue is not simplistic. But you don't have to kill yourself to resolve it. KLM

For help, call New Life Treatment Centers at 1-800-227-LIFE.

Veterans: Share your pain with other vets.

"If Vietnam didn't kill you the first time around, then it won't this time either. Talking about it helps." The speaker had been a "grunt" in Vietnam. He had contemplated suicide when his marriage fell apart and then he'd lost one job after another. Like countless vets, nothing had worked for him since Vietnam. No one understood what he'd been through. No one wanted to listen—until he came to the Vet Center rap group a few weeks before.

Sharing the pain of Vietnam and its aftermath with other vets made a difference in his life. He found people who understood what he'd been through. Healing began through the sharing of stories.

Tragically, more Vietnam vets have taken their own lives than were killed in combat. It need not happen to veterans of other conflicts. Vet Centers are havens for vets. In their rap groups, thousands of vets have rediscovered hope.

Vet Centers are located in every major U.S. city for men and women whose lives have been shattered by war. The alternative to suicide is to rediscover meaning and purpose. A Vet Center is one place to start. WPM

If a part of your soul is still overseas, then it's time for DEROS (for non-vet readers, that's "date of estimated return from overseas"). Look in the white pages of your phone book under Vet Center or call directory assistance in your area code. Go in tomorrow and start to heal your mind and heart. Welcome home!

Get financial advice.

The harassing phone calls wouldn't stop. The bill collectors' voices echoed in Jeff's ears as he rode the bus to work each morning. Jeff couldn't take it anymore. The situation was impossible! On the way home on the bus one night, he began thinking about taking his own life. He thought of a good way to do it, but something held him back. The main drawback was that his suicide would only leave more bills for his wife. He loved her too much to do that to her.

Jeff decided to ask for help.

He had wanted help for a long time, but he didn't know where to go. He didn't have money for a professional counselor, and he didn't realize that community organizations often make counseling available at no charge to people who can't pay. His wife heard a public service announcement on television, wrote down the number, and gave it to Jeff.

Jeff called, made an appointment, and on his lunch hour he began receiving counseling about money matters. Jeff's problems were severe, and they were not solved overnight. But slowly, Jeff learned how to bring manageability into his finances. And he also learned of agencies that offered help with certain emergency needs.

Money problems are stressful but can be solved. JKE

For help with your debts and finances, contact Christian Financial Concepts. CFC has a nationwide network of counselors who volunteer, at no charge, *to help people with debt reduction and budget management. Send a self-addressed, stamped #10 business envelope to CFC, Attn: Counseling Dept., 601 Broad St. S.E., Gainesville, GA 30501. Or call the Consumer Credit Counseling Services at 1-800-388-2227 for a referral to a CCCS office in your area.*

HIV positive? Make a choice to begin.

Maybe you have just received the news that you are HIV positive. Is it the end of your life, or the beginning? If you decide that it is the end of your life, although you may remain healthy for quite a long time, you will feel as though you are already dead. If you decide that it is the beginning, you may feel that you are really living for the first time.

You don't have to be HIV positive to really begin living. It's just that HIV disease rips away that curtain of illusion behind which most people live. It's the illusion that says, yes, there will be a tomorrow, I can do it later, I won't notice, he or she will always be there. If we don't realize that it is an illusion, we will miss out on all that God has to offer us. It is like going to a beautiful dinner party, looking at all the food and thinking we have all the time in the world to eat. Suddenly, without warning, the party is over and we must leave, still hungry, never having eaten.

Being HIV positive can make you stop and think about what you have not yet tasted in life. But you can make the choice to taste it, do it, say it, learn it, love it, ask for it—now. And once you have started to feel alive, you may want to help others who are HIV positive also make a choice to begin.

"A door opens wide when danger and death approach. Somehow when we no longer feel in control, we become available to deeper aliveness."—Richard Moss, in *The Color of Light.* DJ

Buy a copy of The Color of Light *(Hazelden Meditation Series) and take time each day to read a meditation.*

Use your experience with AIDS to help others.

✳ Besides being physically devastating, having AIDS can be
frightening and lonely. Many people who are affected by
AIDS find it impossible to share their thoughts and feelings about
it unless they are talking with a person who has firsthand experience. This is one place that a person living with AIDS can make a
difference. Being involved and connected with other people in an
effort to support, encourage, and educate one another is·a gift that
is given both ways. It gives others hope and understanding and at
the same time can give your life new meaning and direction.

Sharing your experience and encouraging others to share theirs
makes clear the reality that we are all interconnected—who you
are and what you do affects others, just as you are affected by
other people's lives. Our lives often have a ripple effect reaching
farther out and touching more people than we could ever imagine.
You can choose to live fully in the present moment, with all its
pain and love and harshness and grace. By embracing and accepting the "both/and" nature of life, you are embracing and accepting yourself and others.

Even if you are physically unable to get around, *who you are* can
have a tremendous impact on others. Witnessing a life fully lived is
like hearing sweet music—soon you are humming the tune yourself until the notes have found a way into your heart.

"I'm living with AIDS, not dying of AIDS."—Bobbie, a person
with AIDS *(The Color of Light,* Perry Tilleraas). DJ

To get involved in the AIDS community, call or write: National AIDS
Information Clearinghouse, P.O. Box 6003, Rockville, MD 20850
1-800-458-5231, or People with AIDS Coalition, 31 W. 26th St.,
Fifth Floor, New York, NY, 10010, 212-532-0290 or 1-800-828-3280
(toll-free hotline).

FOR INFORMATION ABOUT *AIDS*

National HIV and AIDS Information Service Hotline
  1-800-342-AIDS
  1-800-344-SIDA (Spanish)
  1-800-AIDS-TTY (Hearing impaired)

National AIDS Information Clearinghouse
  1-800-458-5231

AIDS Clinical Trials Information Service
  1-800-TRIALS-A
  1-800-243-7012 (Hearing impaired)

National Institutes of Health Information on AIDS Drug Studies
  1-800-AIDS-NIH

National Sexually Transmitted Diseases Hotline
  1-800-227-8922

DJ

See a therapist.

When I was almost thirty I went through a period of severe doubts. I doubted myself. I doubted my commitment to my marriage. I doubted my choice of career. I felt that I had achieved little in the years since college, and I felt worthless.

One day after work I was waiting at the station for my train home. Watching the huge engine approach, I thought how easy it would be to throw myself onto the track.

I didn't. Instead I called a friend, and she recommended I see a therapist. Thus began some ten months of counseling.

Counseling was a difficult process. It was demanding. It was embarrassing, at times. It was time consuming and expensive. But it was one of the best decisions I ever made.

With the therapist I worked through my doubts and my anger at myself. I discovered gifts and learned to accept weaknesses. I found strategies for coping with stress. I worked through issues left over from childhood. I reaffirmed my marriage and wrestled with the difficult question of whether to have children.

If I had not had therapy, I might have gotten over my depression anyway. It might have slowly abated, but I probably would not have learned much from the experience. And then again, without help, I might not have lived long enough to get over the depression. JG

Read the articles on pages 99, 100, and 101 to learn what kinds of treatment are available. Check your yellow pages or your county's mental health association to learn what is available in your community.

Find the right therapist.

What kind of professional help is best for you? Here are some of the options.

Social workers do much of today's therapy. They are trained in psychology and in assessing the needs of the whole person. They look for the impact of outside stressors such as financial problems, family difficulties, or cultural backgrounds. To do therapy, social workers should have a master's degree in social work (MSW). They may be licensed by the state or by the Academy of Certified Social Workers.

Marriage and family therapists focus on the dynamics of intimate relationships. Look for a therapist who is certified by the American Association of Marriage and Family Therapists; this assures that the person has received adequate training and is professionally qualified. Some states license marriage and family therapists.

Psychologists have a doctoral degree in clinical psychology. Their training focuses on diagnosing and treating emotional problems. They also look for the possibility of organic factors that may contribute to the person's distress. Psychologists are allowed to prescribe medication in some states. They are licensed by the state in which they practice.

Psychiatrists are medical doctors who take additional training in diagnosing and treating mental illness. Some psychiatrists manage symptoms primarily with medication, while others offer both therapy and medication to treat emotional problems. Like other medical doctors, psychiatrists are licensed by their state. JG

Ask trusted friends for recommendations, or look in the yellow pages. It is wise to look for someone who is licensed by your state. Don't forget to trust yourself. If the therapist does not feel right for you, he or she probably isn't.

Enter a short-term treatment program.

✺ I'd never considered that normal people could be so devastated by life's painful experiences that they would consider suicide. . . until it happened to me. My husband's revelation of his addiction devastated our lives. We lost our careers, our finances, our good standing in the community. He was the "identified patient," but I wanted to die.

After he completed his treatment stay the staff suggested that I enter the program to deal with my depression. My time in the hospital wiped away many misconceptions and breathed new life into me. I was taken care of instead of having to always be the one taking care of others. Caring people there listened to me. I made new friends. I ate good meals, rested, exercised, experienced the safety of a set routine, and was relieved of the pressures of everyday life.

With the care of the professional staff, I was able to understand what had driven me to the brink, recognize the effects of my husband's addiction on my life, express my pain, and come up with a plan for my future. CN/CCD

There are various ways to seek professional help when life gets out of hand. However, if life seems totally unbearable, you might benefit from a short-term treatment program.

Some programs, such as Hazelden, offer renewal facilities—a place to get away, relax, and obtain whatever amount of counseling or peer support you want.

People who enter programs such as these are not weak. They are people with the courage to change! Often those who get away from life by getting to treatment find life—a new one.

There are short-term treatment programs in your area. To find out where you can get help, call 1-800-227-LIFE.

Choose the right treatment.

✳ In helping people live more effectively, therapists use different forms of treatment. Here are some options you may be offered:

Long-term individual treatment. A therapist sees one person for an extended period of time, usually several months or years. They explore deep issues in an attempt to treat the underlying causes, not just the symptoms.

Short-term individual treatment. A therapist sees one person for a few weeks or months, focusing immediately on the problem to be solved and establishing concrete goals for treatment.

Group therapy. A therapist works with a group of people focusing on a shared issue such as bereavement, divorce recovery, domestic violence, incest, or parenting.

Marital treatment. A therapist meets with both partners to hear both sides of the problem and to work on strategies for resolution.

Family therapy. A therapist sees all or part of a household together, exploring how the whole family might benefit from changing the family dynamics. This can be helpful even when only one family member seems to be having problems.

Play therapy. A therapist plays with a young child using doll houses, sand boxes, puzzles, and board games in an attempt to encourage the child to express deep-seated emotions.

Peer support groups. Groups of people with similar problems who meet together for encouragement. Not technically a form of therapy, but often very effective. The best-known support groups are those based on the Twelve Step principles of Alcoholics Anonymous.

Most therapy is done in the therapist's office, while some is done at retreats or treatment centers. JG

All of these forms of therapy can be effective. Work with your therapist to find the one, or combination, that best suits your needs.

Find a support group.

☀️A common denominator in many suicides is that the person feels alienated, hopeless, and helpless. He thinks he must face his problem alone and unaided; she wonders if anyone else has ever felt the way she does.

If you feel this way, think about joining a support group.

A support group is not a form of professional counseling. It is simply a group of people with a similar concern who have agreed to meet with each other regularly and to help each other as needed. The concern that unites them can be almost anything. There are support groups for people with chemical dependencies, eating problems, various illnesses, unusual family situations, similar hobbies—you name it, you'll find a support group for it.

In a support group people understand your feelings, because they are dealing with similar issues.

You no longer feel alienated, because you have made contact with people who truly understand.

Seeing what has worked for other people, you begin to feel hopeful.

Encouraged by group members, you learn where help can be found and what you can do to help yourself.

When you become part of a support group, you discover that other members need you as much as you need them. Each person in the group, including you, has something different to offer, something that matters in the lives of the other group members. Knowing that you are needed gives you added strength to go on. CN

To track down the group you want, try a local hospital, crisis center, church, talk radio station, or treatment center. Treatment Centers Magazine *compiles a list of support groups for some areas; contact them at P.O. Box 401651, Dallas, TX 75240. Or find another person who shares your concern and start a support group of your own!*

Work through the Twelve Step recovery process at least once.

The Twelve Step Program, originally developed by Alcoholics Anonymous to deal with alcoholism, has proved to be a valuable tool in dealing with all kinds of addictions, compulsions, and codependent behaviors. In fact, many of the problems that drive people to thoughts of suicide respond favorably to the Twelve Steps.

When people get to the point of thinking about suicide, they often feel powerless over something in their life. Their life seems out of control, unmanageable. Often some form of addiction has a hold on them; it seems impossible to break. They are in tremendous pain. Suicide becomes an attractive option at this point, but it's not the only option. Many have come to this point and found it to be the starting point for a whole new life.

The first step toward recovery for those struggling with addictive/compulsive behavior is to admit that they have no power within themself to make the changes they need to make. This is, in essence, Step One of the Twelve Step Program. The rest of the steps build on this profound insight. Followed carefully, one at a time, they help the person learn to stand on his or her own feet again.

A person who works through the entire Twelve Steps at least once has a powerful tool against suicide and for recovery. Though some problems—grief, for example—need a different approach, most people benefit from working through the Twelve Steps no matter what drove them to despair. It's worth a try. CN

Check the white pages of your phone book for the number of the local chapter of Alcoholics Anonymous (AA), or phone the public library or the office of one of the larger churches in your area to find out what other Twelve Step programs are available.

Check with a physician or two.

✳ Physical problems may contribute to your feelings of hopelessness. A visit to your doctor can uncover them.

A woman I had seen in counseling sessions for a number of months suddenly called me for an emergency appointment. She was desperate. She saw life as completely hopeless.

Fortunately, I *knew* she was emotionally stable. But I found out she had just made a drastic change in her hormone medication. I convinced her that her problem was probably hormones.

I referred her to a gynecologist, who adjusted her medication. She has been fine ever since. Yet conceivably she could have given up if medical care had not been expertly and readily administered.

Many people have physical problems that create emotional symptoms: hormonal imbalances after childbirth, PMS, menopause, low blood sugar, thyroid imbalances, and diseases of the liver, for example. Even antidepressants or antianxiety medication can cause depression, if the wrong drugs or doses are given.

Always consider the interplay of body, mind, and spirit when dealing with emotional problems. As Charles Spurgeon said over a century ago: "Certain bodily maladies are fruitful foundations of despondency. . . . Where in body and mind there are predisposing causes to lowness of spirit, it is no marvel if in dark moments the heart succumbs to them. The wonder in many cases is . . . how some keep at their work at all and still wear a smile upon their countenances."

And don't forget—get a second opinion, especially when you are dissatisfied or your condition is diagnosed as terminal. ERS

Check with your doctor. If that doesn't work, check with another doctor, perhaps a specialist. Aggressively monitor your own diagnosis and treatment. Remember, no doctor is infallible. Don't give up until you get results.

See if you need chemical therapy.

Depression has two sides.

One is the emotional side. It is recognized by a sense of hopelessness or despair, loss of pleasure in life, feelings of worthlessness or guilt, and thoughts of suicide.

The other side is biochemical. Chemical imbalances can lead to eating problems, fatigue, inability to concentrate, restlessness or listlessness, insomnia or sleeping too much.

The two sides work together. An emotionally based depression can lead to biochemical disturbances. Physical malfunctions can lead to emotional disturbances. Treating just one side of depression sometimes is not enough.

Some practitioners treat depressed clients using antidepressant medication, including tricyclic antidepressants, monoamine oxidase (MAO) inhibitors, and fluoxetine (Prozac). These medications can be effective in raising a person's energy level and mood, regulating sleeping or eating patterns, and alleviating anxiety. But if the depression is also emotionally based, and that is not addressed, then the depression may return or fail to abate.

Other professionals treat depression with therapy to get at the source of the problem that originally sent the depressed person to them. But if the biochemical imbalance is not dealt with, the therapy may have limited or temporary effect.

Not all people need chemical therapy. But some do. Monitor medication carefully. Certain drugs given to treat depression or anxiety can also cause depression if not suited for the client. Also, check to see if the drug prescribed for you is addictive. JG

If you believe your depression is being treated halfway, ask your doctor or therapist what more can be done. Or find an agency that will help you find treatment.

Find out why you are tired.

✳ Fatigue and depression are often closely related. Tired people work less effectively. They often feel dissatisfied and restless. They find it hard to deal with complex problems, and they are easily upset by trivial things. Tired people are often irritable and critical. They lack joy and spontaneity. Fatigue can make life look pretty dismal!

But it's possible to find relief for fatigue.

Some fatigue is *organic.* It is the result of a disease or deficiency, although the tired person may not realize there is a physical problem. If you are chronically tired, get a physical examination. The doctor may uncover something that can be easily fixed.

Some fatigue is *constitutional.* Not everyone has the same energy level. People who work or play too vigorously, too long, or too often may go beyond their natural physical limits. We live in a busy world, but we have to know and respect our individual limits. Keep track of your schedule for a week and see if you are trying to pack too much into a day.

Some fatigue is *psychological* or *spiritual.* Inappropriate relationships, self-defeating ways of acting, energy-draining attitudes—these can all lead to chronic tiredness. As with physical disease, we may not recognize the problem without expert help. If your fatigue persists even though you are physically healthy and sensibly scheduled, make an appointment with a counselor to see if you can get to the root of the problem. RG

Start fighting fatigue today by making an appointment for a complete physical, with laboratory tests.

Learn to manage chronic pain.

Pain. Raw, aching stiffness. I've known it for several years since the accident. It's hard to remember what life was like when I didn't hurt.

When doctors told me I'd have to learn to live with pain, I didn't believe it. They were supposed to have answers. They were supposed to fix things.

Forever seemed a cruel, unjust sentence. I contemplated the future. My life revolved around appointments with doctors, physical therapy, and rehabilitation at home. Days, months, years loomed like a bottomless abyss.

Chronic pain, whether physical or emotional, takes its toll, wearing at the very core of our being. Many nights I felt so exhausted I wondered how I'd face another day, much less a whole lifetime.

I began looking at each day as only a twenty-four-hour segment. "I can handle the pain for today," I told myself. I refused to dwell on words like *forever* or *the rest of my life*. Sometimes I had to take one hour at a time. I mourned losses: brisk early morning walks, the wind in my face when I jogged, hikes on mountain trails.

Days became a series of more manageable steps rather than a life sentence. Weeks stretched into gradual acceptance, focusing on what I could still do. I found that God's grace was sufficient— one day at a time. DK

Focus on today, this moment. Live in the present. Not tomorrow, next week, or next year. Enjoy the wonders of today: the sound of wind in the trees, children laughing on their way to school, sunshine streaming through a window. You may be surprised by God's grace.

Find relief from your physical pain.

✳ For some who experience physical pain, relief can be achieved in numerous ways.

According to specialist Dr. Matthew Connolly, "total pain" includes mental, social, spiritual, and physical pain. He says, "Failure to remember this complexity is one of the most common reasons why patients fail to achieve adequate symptomatic relief" (*Issues in Law & Medicine* 4 [1989]:497-507).

Physical pain relief has become increasingly sophisticated. For example, the recently developed patient-controlled analgesic pump allows a patient to dispense needed doses of narcotic pain-relievers into the bloodstream, even at home.

Pain relief can also be achieved through spiritual or emotional means. Dr. Richard Lamerton, a hospice director, says: "I remember one lady whose arthritis was a source of perpetual suffering. She was bedbound, and she depressed even the other patients near her. A combination of antidepressants and knitting scarves for me (using specially fat needles that she could, reluctantly, in spite of deformed fingers, hold) transformed her into a cheerful, almost pain-free lady who kept a copy of *Lolita* surreptitiously under her pillow. Her actual painkillers were not changed" (*Ibid.* 2 [1987]:379-390). MSG

With your doctor, brainstorm possible treatments for physical pain. A pain clinic or stress-management workshop might offer further insight into the nonphysical causes of your discomfort. Ask your hospital social worker for recommendations.

Find a doctor who will aggressively treat physical pain.

Most people who experience excruciating pain entertain thoughts of suicide. Faced with endless pain, few of us would not consider death a preferable alternative. But help for those in pain is available, if doctors are courageous enough to use it.

Recent years have seen a tremendous outcry against the illicit use of drugs. Unfortunately, too often the legitimate use of drugs has also suffered. Doctors, fearing that a patient might become dependent on narcotics and require ever-increasing doses to produce the desired relief, may avoid altogether the use of strong pain killers. While drug addiction should be avoided wherever possible, it makes no sense to worry about dependency when the only other choice is excruciating pain or death.

If you are thinking of suicide because of pain, look for a doctor who will take your pain seriously and respond with appropriate treatment. There are methods of pain treatment that prevent pain while preserving a patient's alertness and ability to relate normally to the world. Some of these involve narcotics and sedatives; some use biofeedback or electronic pain devices. New approaches are always being researched.

Patients have the right to seek such aggressive treatment. If your current doctor will not provide it, look for one who will. JG

In many communities, a hospice will have information about doctors who make patients' comfort a high priority. Look in your yellow pages under hospice, *or phone the National Hospice Organization (Virginia) at 703-243-5900 to find the number of a hospice near you. Other potential sources of information include a physician referral service or the local office of the American Cancer Society.*

Learn your rights as a patient.

✳ Chances are, at some point in your illness, you have felt that you lack control over your life. An uninvited guest—this disease—has set up housekeeping in your body. To add insult to injury, you face the bureaucratic and often impersonal health-care system. You may feel confused about your role in this high-tech environment.

Now is not the time to give in passively and let the system control you. Learn your rights as a patient, and practice them.

The code of patients' rights was formulated by the American Hospital Association and has become law in ten states. Five of these rights may be especially relevant in situations of terminal illness. You have the right to:

* receive considerate and respectful care
* receive information about your illness, the course of treatment, and the prospects for recovery in terms that you can understand
* receive as much information about any proposed treatment or procedure as you may need in order to give informed consent or to refuse this course of treatment (except in emergencies)
* participate actively in decisions regarding medical care; to the extent permitted by law, this includes the right to refuse treatment
* have all patients' rights apply to the person who may have legal responsibility to make medical care decisions on your behalf. MSG

For a full list of patients' rights, contact your hospital's patient representative or admitting department. Do you need to make changes to ensure that your rights are respected? Consider how to make those changes.

Communicate your desires for future medical treatment.

Recent developments in medical technology generate both hope and fear. The hope is that new medical procedures can extend and enhance our life. The fear is that these developments will be misused to prolong our dying process at great costs. Be sure your desires for medical treatment will be carried out by taking time now to communicate them.

Two documents have received much publicity. The *Living Will* allows a person to ask that certain measures be taken if he or she becomes incapable of making medical decisions. The *durable power of attorney for health care* (DPA) allows an individual to appoint someone to make medical decisions if the patient can't.

Every American has the legal right to say no to any form of medical treatment. To ensure you don't lose this right simply because you are too sick to refuse, exercise it in advance. Whatever you decide, you, your primary physician, and a close family member or friend should discuss these questions for starters:

* Who should make my medical decisions if I cannot?
* If I become incompetent, what role do I want my family to play? My physician? My pastor? Others?
* What treatments and care do I consider imperative? Unnecessary? Under what circumstances?
* Does my age, physical condition, financial status, or family situation alter the measures I want taken at the end of life?
* What about living in a nursing home? Dying in a hospice, at home, or in the hospital? MSG

For information on these documents, send a self-addressed, stamped envelope to Americans United for Life, 343 S. Dearborn St., Suite 1804, Chicago, IL 60604. Make an appointment to talk with your doctor and a family member about your wishes.

Take advantage of hospice care.

☀ If you are terminally ill, you are confronting despair, pain, and deep uncertainty. You may have thought it seems pointless to live only to suffer. For people who are dying, hospice care offers a unique program of pain relief and counseling. It affirms life, even as it acknowledges that death is close. And for the most part, it soundly rejects suicide and assisted suicide.

Some hospice programs are located in hospitals, while others have separate buildings. If a terminally ill patient wishes to remain at home, a hospice can provide visiting nurses and volunteers.

Hospice care is much different from ordinary medical care. If you are being treated in a hospital, the main goal of treatment is to cure you. For a terminally ill patient, that goal does not apply. Yet there is much that can be done. In the care of hospice professionals, you will receive medication to ease physical pain. And you will have counselors, nurses, and chaplains available to help you and your family cope with the emotional trauma you face.

Jeanne Brenneis, chaplain at Hospice of Northern Virginia, explains, "In my counseling, I try to nudge people to see that even in the despair of knowing that their life is ending, there are bright spots. . . . We try to help people be fully alive while they are dying—to the very end." The hospice Brenneis represents has been active since 1977. In that time, it has helped thousands of terminally ill patients cope with dying. It has also helped their families cope with bereavement. BLS

There are more than 1,700 hospice programs active in the United States today. Information about these programs is available from the National Hospice Organization, 1901 North Moore Street, Suite 901, Arlington, VA 22209; 703-243-5900. A book on the hospice philosophy is The Hospice Alternative: A New Context for Death & Dying *by Anne Munley (New York: Basic Books, 1986).*

Make plans to help people remember you.

My neighbor Julie, an artist, knew her days were limited when the cancer kept growing despite aggressive treatment. So she planned her memorial service. The day of the service, each guest received a hand-lettered bulletin adorned by an exquisite drawing by Julie. Even in her death she was creative.

Those who know death is imminent have the opportunity to make use of it. Planning your memorial service is one way to make your death have an impact. This gathering of loved ones may be the catalyst to begin healing a family rift. At a memorial service, hearts are often open to the moving of God.

As you feel ready, begin to plan your service:

* Decide what you want your obituary to include. Don't stick to bare facts. Include special memories like the time your friends threw an "over the hill" birthday party for you, or your pride at seeing your children graduate from college.

* Choose music that reflects your personality and the thoughts you want to convey. Music does not have to be mournful. If you wish, you can choose praise choruses, hymns, an appropriate popular song.

* Talk with your pastor about the message. This is an excellent opportunity to explain your faith clearly to those at the service. You may even want to tape record a message in your own words.

* Decide where the service will be held. If the funeral home is dark and foreboding, consider an alternative—a forest preserve, a garden, a sunny churchyard. MSG

Ask yourself: What would I like to accomplish with my memorial service? Start a notebook with ideas. Share it with a friend.

Find a mentor.

Dealing with teen suicide, educator Thomas K. Edwards says that schools "can provide young people with reasons for wanting to live by thoughtfully 'mentoring' each youngster" (*Education Digest*, March 1989). A mentor is an informal adviser who helps the student through hard situations.

Adults can benefit from mentors too. Especially in tough times, we all need someone to be there for us, to help us see things straight.

Look for a person of wisdom and maturity, someone you respect, but also someone you can be honest with. It might be a close friend, someone you work with, an acquaintance from your church or community. (It probably should not be a family member.)

When you find such a person, ask him or her to be your mentor for a period of six months or a year. Say something like this: "I'm going through some really difficult times right now, and I need someone who can keep me thinking straight. Over the next six months I want to be able to call you when I need someone to talk to, and I want you to check up on me if you haven't heard from me."

Warning: The person may say no. If so, look for someone else.

"The goal of . . . any potential rescuer is to broaden the suicidal person's perspective," writes Edwin Shneidman, founder of the American Association of Suicidology (*Psychology Today*, March 1987). "Life is often a choice among many unpleasant possibilities, and the goal is to select the least unpleasant one." A mentor can help you see straight to do that. RP

Start by making a short list of possible mentors. If you are connected with a church, talk to the pastor about this. If not, try asking your doctor to recommend someone.

Get to know the *who.*

※ "He who has a *why* to live can bear with almost any *how*," wrote Friedrich Nietzsche.

Anna Morgan, age seventy-six, was legally blind and barely able to walk. She had no close friends or family and lived alone. A suicide attempt reflected her inner emptiness and pain. She began to verbally express both as she was recovering in the hospital's psychiatric ward. "I want to leave this nice world. Nobody loves me, needs me, or wants me," she told the nurse.

Exploration of Anna's needs and feelings uncovered deep spiritual despair. "God? What God? There is no God."

Sarah Blackburn, age ninety-five, lay confined to her bed in a nursing home. Contractures contorted her frail body. Chronic pain was a way of life. Every weekend people from a nearby church would visit the nursing home, conduct a worship service, and then spend time visiting the residents who were bedridden. They read from the Bible to Sarah each week.

One weekend Sarah told a visitor she had survived a concentration camp. "I never understood the suffering, but there was God. He got me through. He was my light."

When the whys don't make sense or are absent, suffering can still be borne and have meaning. As William Hulme wrote in *Dialogue in Despair,* "He who knows the *who* can bear with almost any *how,* even though he doesn't know the *why.*"

Anna Morgan and Sarah Blackburn didn't have a *why.* Sarah Blackburn didn't need one. SF

Get to know the who. *Read Margaret Clarkson's* Grace Grows Best in Winter *(Eerdmans). Read the book of Isaiah in the Bible and discover God, the One who gives hope in the midst of suffering.*

CHAPTER FIVE

Reasons to Choose Life

*T*he previous three sections in this book contained things to do. This section touches on reasons to do them. The whys. Some people say we shouldn't ask why when something bad happens.

Well, let me tell you, I ask why. I ask it and ask it. Then I ask it again. I've learned one thing: never let anyone tell you how to grieve. There's no rule book. It's your game. Besides, you hear too many conflicting stories: Feel more, feel less. Be strong, be weak.

Blah. Blah. Blah. It's my grief, and I'll cry if and when I want to. (I cry a lot.)

Reasons to live are a way of asking why.

I can't tell you the whys about the bad that has happened in my life. But I can give you some perspective on them.

When I was actively using drugs and alcohol, I attempted suicide many times. Once, police dragged me down from a bridge I was threatening to jump from. Once, they broke open my apartment door, pulled my head out of the oven, and turned off the gas.

Many times, I woke up from a drug overdose, saw the life support equipment attached to my body and felt enraged that I was still alive.

"Why didn't I die?"

I'm not sure. But when I was twenty-six, on the rolling lawn outside the chemical dependency unit of Wilmar State Hospital, I had a spiritual awakening. And I got sober.

When I bottomed out on my codependency, seven years after I got sober, and began wishing for death, I wondered why. I wondered *why* I felt so miserable. I wondered *why* my marriage wasn't working. I wondered *why* I felt so bad so much of the time. I wondered, *Why me?*

I called a suicide hotline one day and told a stranger, "I want to kill myself. But don't worry, I won't. Too many people need me."

But I didn't want to live, and I didn't understand *why.*

Years later, I wrote down some ideas that helped me recover from codependency. The book became a best-seller.

I've asked why a lot lately. I ask it whenever I want. I don't have an answer yet. I don't understand.

But I've learned that understanding the purpose usually doesn't come until later, after I've gone through whatever experience I'm facing.

I wish I could tell you that my spiritual beliefs have made everything all better. They haven't. There is one part of me that has firm beliefs, that knows I can trust God and the higher purpose for my life, even when it doesn't look like I can.

But there is another part too. My human part. My feelings. My doubt, rage, fear, and mistrust. The part of me that misses Shane. The part of me that feels enraged that my daughter has to go through what she's experiencing.

Gradually, these two parts of myself are meeting. My doctor is a wonderful man. He's not just a doctor; he's a healer. He has stood by me through the process I've gone through, supporting not just my body, but my emotions, my mind, and my spirit.

"Life has no meaning," I told Dr. Bill one day. "It's stupid. Senseless. *There's no point.* Even the good things we do, the things we accomplish, really don't mean much. It's all trivial. And dull. And it scares me that life has no meaning."

Dr. Bill listened quietly.

"Is this part of my process?" I asked. "This 'life has no meaning' thing?"

He nodded. "It's a gate you must walk through to find meaning," he responded. "Don't force purpose. Don't force meaning. Let it find you."

I'm learning that my humanity is not separate or in opposition to my spirituality. It is connected, a necessary part.

Not only can we trust God, we can trust and be gentle with ourself.

Read through this "Reasons to Choose Life" section. Listen to what people have to say. But understand that these are *their* reasons to live. Then find yours. It might be *you,* your children, your work, *love,* money, or your spiritual beliefs—or some of each. You may already *have* your reason to live . . . and all you need is to open your eyes and recognize it. You may be in deep pain because you've lost some, most, or all of your reason.

Ask why. Get mad. Then go outside, stand on your porch, open your arms, look up at the heavens, and scream, "God—give me a reason to live."

Then keep your head up. Your heart open. And see what happens next.

TWELVE REASONS TO LIVE

This list was written in a psychiatric hospital by a woman who, two weeks earlier, had attempted suicide.

1. Because I *deserve* to live
2. Because I want to look at the sky
3. Because I need to laugh
4. So I can write letters to God
5. So I can eat pizza and popcorn
6. So I can hug my son
7. So I can look in the mirror
8. So I can run in sneakers
9. So I can jump in a puddle
10. So I can wear bows in my hair
11. So I can sing in the shower
12. So I can hear crickets chirping

MLB

You are taking a journey into the unknown.

☀ The starship *Enterprise* and suicide both represent treks into the unknown, each leading to a distinctly different destination.

One explores strange and unusual places in search of *life*, journeying boldly where no one has gone before. The other takes its passengers on a voyage of self-destruction. Its mission: to explore unorthodox and unalterable schemes that ultimately lead to *death*. Others may have traveled its path, but they do not return to talk of its mysteries.

When an event of such significance occurs that it brings you to the point of considering suicide, and you reject that decision in favor of life, you buy a ticket on your own starship *Enterprise*.

You have just chosen to explore strange and unusual places in search of life, hope, and spiritual growth. What will you find? What mysteries will be revealed to you? What will you learn?

How will your experience benefit others, benefit humankind?

What will you learn about the intricate and powerful workings of God?

What will you discover about your purpose, your destiny?

How will you contribute to the future, and destiny, of humankind?

I cannot answer these questions for you, my friend. I am just beginning to fathom them for myself. But this I know: if you have despaired to the point of suicide, then have chosen life, you have chosen a mysterious journey that will bring you answers to all of the above.

If you hurt that badly, your experience is *that* important—to you, and the rest of the world.

Stick around, and you will discover why. SC/KLM

Sit back, buckle up, and embrace the journey you've undertaken.

You're in good company.

First quotation: "I am now the most miserable man living. To remain as I am is impossible. I must die or be better."

Second quotation: "So if you are going to deal thus with me, please kill me at once."

Third quotation: "It is enough; now, O Lord, take away my life."

Three quotations, probably from three losers. Right? Who else would be so down in the dumps that they actually wanted God to take life from them? Must have been three who were mentally deranged, no good to society. Right? What could have made people say things so desperate? They must have been worthless people. Right?

Wrong!

The first quotation is from Abraham Lincoln.

The second quotation is from Moses, the great leader of Israel.

The third quotation is from the prophet Elijah.

Do great things come from people who at one time in their lives have hit rock bottom?

Yes, they do. CCD

Trusting in Him who can go with me, and remain with you, and be everywhere for good, let us confidently hope that all will yet be well. ◆ Abraham Lincoln, farewell address, Springfield, Illinois

Someone who's been there says life is worth it.

This is an actual letter to someone who was about to commit suicide from someone who didn't:

I don't even know you, but I know something about the way you feel.

People have told you that life really *is* worth living. I know. They told me that too.

Others say that you are being selfish and not thinking about all the people you would hurt. I know. They told me that too.

And what about the great line, "You're going to learn so much from this experience"? I know. They told me that too.

How can they know what they're talking about unless they have been in your shoes? You are in so much pain that it seems as if life *isn't* worth living. I know. I thought that too.

You probably don't care if it might hurt others. I know. I was prepared to hurt others too.

And you probably are convinced life will never get better. I know. I was convinced too.

They don't know. But I do. Hang on. Please hang on. I want you to write a letter to someone else some day. You're *not* alone. I know. I'm still here too! CCD

Each man can interpret another's experience only by his own.
◆ Henry David Thoreau

A daughter's love letter to Dad

✵ This is from a forty-seven-year-old woman to her father, who turns eighty-two this week. He's been feeling bad about himself—about various decisions he made, or failed to make, during his lifetime. His eyes are weak; his daughter typed her message all in capital letters to make it easier for him to read. We'll print it in caps and lowercase here, but the thoughts are the same:

"Dear Dad,

"I don't know how to write this without making it sound gooey or like a lecture. I just hope I can make you understand what I want to say, and understand that it comes out of love and concern for you.

"From what I hear from Mother it sounds as though you are deeply depressed—please don't throw this letter down yet. It bothers me very much to hear this because sometimes I think that emotional pain can be harder to bear than physical pain. At least with physical pain you can point to it and it's something for which a doctor can prescribe treatment.

"Emotional pain is sometimes something that you can deny exists, something that you don't absolutely *have* to get treatment for. But it can eat away at you as badly as any dread disease can. It can destroy your desire to do anything for yourself, it can begin to make you believe that you are not worthwhile and, for this reason, no one in your life could really care about you, and that nothing in your life has any merit.

"I want to tell you that your family loves you now, always has, and always will—no matter how you feel about yourself now.

"You are a big part of most of my favorite childhood memories.

"I enjoyed the Sunday car rides (despite the occasional car sickness!), the almost weekly movies with popcorn and jujubes, and how you used to walk up to the 'Balcony Is Closed' sign, unhook the red velvet rope and walk upstairs with your family and no one stopped us.

"My all-time favorite childhood memory is of a time when I was getting ready for bed on a summer evening. The sky was still light and you said, 'Get dressed, we're going to Riverview.'

"Riverview, a land of roller coasters, the ferris wheel, the merry-go-round! I don't think I ever said anything to my own children as wonderful and magical and that will have the lasting impact that those words had on me. I'll never forget anything about that moment—that second chance at life at the close of the day!

"So much of who I am now is wrapped up in you and Mother. Some of it is a reaction to things I didn't like in my life. This is normal in every generation. I'm sure you did the same. Much of what I do now is the same as the way you did things because as I was growing up those things were important to me.

"The whole point of all this is that however you feel about the direction your life has taken, I personally have some very good feelings about the past, about the way I grew up. Not everything was rosy, but we learn from the bad times and there was a whole lot more good than bad.

"As far as career choices—don't we all wish we had made some different choices. But we are what we are and you had a good job. You made a few friends, supported your family, and if you didn't retire a millionaire, well, neither do most people.

"I wish there were a way for you to forgive yourself for roads not taken, and a way for you to try to look at who you are and what you have as good and worthwhile.

"I know you have some physical limitations now, but can you take stock of what you can do for yourself, so that you can continue to enjoy a good life? Because you earned it and because you deserve it and because you are worth the time, money and effort it would take to help yourself.

"For instance (and forgive me if it's a sensitive subject), can you go and get your hearing tested and get a hearing aid? I sometimes want to say things to you and I don't because I'm afraid you won't hear and understand. I think this must cut you off from so much when people hesitate to really talk to you because of this. As a matter of fact, this is why I'm writing this letter. I want to tell you how I feel but I'm afraid you might misunderstand what I'm trying to say.

"For your birthday you told Mother to tell us 'not to give you a birthday party or to even send a dollar-fifty card.' I want to tell you that I feel you're worth a *two-dollar* card *plus* a party!

"And every morning when you get up, it might be a house of mirrors, a roller coaster, or a ride on the carousel. But it's a new day. So 'Get dressed, you're going to Riverview!'

"Love,

"Your daughter."

By Bob Greene, reprinted by permission from the Chicago Tribune.

You are unique.

I remember the very moment when I first realized how unique each individual is. I was a small child when, looking intently at my mother's face, I realized that there would never be another her. I memorized the laugh lines around her eyes and the soft brown wisps of hair at her temples. No one else would ever look just like her. No one else would ever act just like her. She was unique.

Each of us has our own individual physical appearance. Each of us has a unique emotional and intellectual and spiritual makeup. There will never be another you. There will never be another me.

Furthermore, each of us has our own job to do. We are here in this place, at this time, for a specific reason. God has called only you to your task. He has called only me to mine. Nobody else can do your job for you or my job for me.

You cannot be replaced or duplicated. Your value is not in what you might become, who you have been, or even what you do. Your value comes simply from *you* being *you.* ERS/KLM

> *Who is it that says most? which can say more*
> *Than this rich praise—that you alone are you?*
> ◆ William Shakespeare, *Sonnet 84*

Your life is intertwined with others who love you.

Terminal cancer. The words played through Denise's mind like a broken record. She cried softly into her pillow so she wouldn't wake her husband.

She had found the lump in her breast during her last months of pregnancy. Fear robbed her of her joy. Two weeks after the emergency C-section and delivery of her baby daughter, Denise entered the hospital again for a radical mastectomy.

Chemotherapy ravaged her, leaving her skin sallow, her head bald. Doctors suggested she discontinue treatment.

Denise found herself thinking of ways to end the nightmare. With a slight turn of the steering wheel while alone . . . no one would know it wasn't an accident.

Then she thought of her family. Her four sons and newborn daughter. Her husband. They all loved her. They needed her.

Denise chose life. She found a doctor who treated her illness aggressively. She sought the help of a psychiatrist for her depression. That was six years ago. Denise has watched her oldest son graduate from high school and her youngest child climb on the school bus for kindergarten. For Denise, life is a precious gift. DK

I learned that it is possible for us to create light and sound and order within us, no matter what calamity may befall us in the outer world. ◆ Helen Keller

You can learn to give and receive in new ways.

✳ A twenty-three-year-old woman lost control of her car one night on a slippery road. The car overturned, she snapped her neck, and she was paralyzed from the chin down. She couldn't talk, move her head, or breathe without a machine. Her children were five and six years old.

What made her decide to keep going? "I still have lots of love to give," she said. "I'm learning a new way to give that love."

Although she could not do the physical work of parenting her children, she could still communicate with them and be in a relationship with them. Every day after school they visited her in the hospital. They climbed on her lap or sat on her bed and showed off their finger paintings, paper kites, and spelling tests. She praised, corrected, encouraged, and simply loved them. They learned to read her lips, push her wheelchair, and comb her hair.

The roles of parent and child remained the same, although now her children were giving her more physical care than she gave them. "It's hard for me not to bathe and dress them, and it's hard for me to let somebody else bathe and dress me," she said. "But we're all learning to give and receive love in different ways than before." DJ

Love is patient; love is kind. . . . It does not rejoice in wrongdoing, but rejoices in the truth. It bears all things, believes all things, hopes all things, endures all things. Love never ends. . . . And now faith, hope, and love abide, these three; and the greatest of these is love.
◆ St. Paul in 1 Corinthians 13

It's OK to need people.

※ "I remember my grandfather after a stroke had stripped away his ability to talk, to read, to hear, and to understand. His use-lessness lay heavy on him—he had always been an impatient man. But people in his small Kansas farm town loved him because of what showed on his face," said Tim. "Something you saw in him made your heart glow. I cannot explain it, though I felt it, and I know others felt it too. 'He has so much love,' people said."

No matter what our circumstances, we can always maintain our ability to give love—to deliberately choose to love people, to be a channel, an instrument, a mirror of greater love, God's love.

Perhaps the most difficult, challenging part of being afflicted—whether that affliction is emotional, physical, or both—isn't main-taining our ability to love others. It is becoming vulnerable enough to allow ourselves to receive love.

Many of us have spent our lives caring for, and giving to, others. We may have prided ourself on our fierce independence and on not *needing* people, at least not significantly enough to let it show.

Suddenly, we may find ourself helpless as a turtle on its back—needing emotional support, physical presence, someone to hold our hand; maybe needing someone to bathe us, dress us, care for us, or help us go to the bathroom. Even with all our strength, deter-mination, and wisdom, and with God holding our hand, we find ourself needing *people*, too.

Perhaps that is the hardest, and most important, lesson we have to learn. TS/KLM

The community, moreover, may need its aged and dependent, its sick and its dying, and the virtues which they sometimes evince—the virtues of humility, courage, and patience—just as much as the community needs the virtues of justice and love manifest in the agents of care. ◆ William F. May, *The Christian Century*

Someone needs you.

✳ I stared at the bottle of tranquilizers, wondering if there was enough to do the job. I wouldn't want to fail at my attempt and end up brain-damaged.

The list of reasons why not to kill myself ran through my mind, as it had several times before. It was boring. I knew it by heart. *Situation is temporary. May get better tomorrow. Lots of people have gone through this. Somehow, it'll work out for good.*

Nothing touched my soul, until I came to the last one.

Someone needs you.

I knew that. I even knew the correct list of names of who needed me: my son, my family members, my friends, strangers I hadn't met yet that I could help, volunteer organizations, and God.

Great list. Accurate. Right on. But it didn't do it. Yes, I cared. But other people "needing" me just didn't get it. Not now.

"You forgot someone," the list said.

One year later, when I sat in some friends' living room, discussing the incident with them, they asked me what had made me decide not to end my life.

"Probably a little bit of a lot of reasons," I said. "But the strongest thing that kept me going was the cry of one person that needed me—needed me to be strong, needed me to see this thing through to the end, needed me to see how it would work out, needed me to stick around and see what possible benefits could come from this."

"Who's that?" they asked.

"Me," I said. KLM

Make a list of the people who need you, and the people who would be affected by your death. Put your name on the list too, then keep it where you can see it.

Somebody needs something you can give.

"There's an Officer Ripley inside who sure could use a hug."

135

Your pain can be transformed into healing for others.

Elizabeth stood outside the emergency room of a large hospital. She breathed the cool evening air, trying to comprehend. It was Saturday. She had seen a few patients, then gone home for a quiet dinner. Then the phone rang. Her mother, sister, and aunt had been in an accident. All three were in intensive care.

This is what you read about in the papers and wonder how you could endure it, Elizabeth thought. *Now, it's happening to me.*

A few days later, after her mother's funeral, she found comfort in Robert Frost's words: "I have promises to keep, and miles to go before I sleep." She was suffering deeply, but instinctively knew that what she was going through would help her become more compassionate and understanding with other people whose lives were shattered.

In the movie *The Doctor,* William Hurt plays a surgeon in a large hospital who suddenly finds himself in the role of patient. He has developed throat cancer and may lose his voice, die, or both.

As the movie progresses, he watches the courage of a dying woman who could not beat her illness. He watches the sometimes cold and unthinking treatment delivered by hospital personnel.

Eventually, Hurt beats his cancer and returns to his position. But he is no longer the same. He treats people differently; he teaches other doctors to treat people differently—insisting that they become patients, before they can be doctors.

When we have lived through great pain, we can never be as we were before. But we can allow our pain to be transformed into healing and love that will touch the world. ERS

Although the world is full of suffering, it is also full of the overcoming of it. ◆ Helen Keller

You can help others—and yourself.

Spiritually based self-help programs such as Alcoholics Anonymous long ago recognized not only the virtue, but the self-healing benefits available by reaching out and helping someone who has the same problem as us. Newly sober alcoholics who craved a drink were instructed to find another suffering alcoholic and "carry the message of hope" to him or her.

There were pitfalls to this process, of course. But overall, the process of reaching out to someone with the same problem we have works. It may truly benefit the other person, and it usually helps us.

This concept is not restricted to alcoholics. It can work among people grieving the loss of a loved one, cancer patients, or people facing addictions or out-of-control behaviors in any area of their lives.

And we don't have to wait until we "get it all together" to help others, either. Reaching out to others in a healthy way, while we are doing what we need to help ourselves, can begin *now.*

Sharing experience, strength, and hope—no matter how minuscule that experience, strength, and hope may appear to us at the moment—makes them grow larger.

Reaching out helps us formulate our new beliefs and gives us needed respites from focusing on our pain.

Some people suggest that we teach what we know best; others say we find ourselves by teaching what we most need to learn. If hope is what you need most, try giving some away. ERS/KLM

To act in faith . . . is to venture beyond what sight will warrant; to let go the obvious and tangible supports to which we might cling within a closely bounded field, and to commit ourselves to principles which sense cannot certify, to lines of action on which sense will not accompany us, to a sustaining power which sense has never promised. ◆ Bishop Paget

God is forgiving.

The man had spent twenty-four years involved in moral atrocities. Now in his middle forties, he realized the futility of his life. He didn't speak the word "sin," but he had come to a realization of himself, his past. Suicide seemed the only option.

"Give me a reason not to do it," he said, "but don't tell me it's wrong, because everything else I've ever done has been wrong." The minister listened to him silently. "You don't know what it's like," the man continued, "because you've spent your life working for God. Where does that leave me?"

"The shepherd in Jesus' story leaves the ninety-nine sheep and goes after the lost one. The father in the parable gives a party for the runaway son, not for the faithful son. It leaves you in a better position than I," the minister replied. "After all, the Bible is in your favor."

The woman sat on the edge of her chair, looking down at the floor. She couldn't look the counselor in the eye. She couldn't look anyone in the eye. She had run from her life for years—staying one step ahead of the feelings.

Now, she couldn't run anymore.

"I've been a prostitute. Slept with old men and young men. Degraded my body. Had two abortions. I've stole from people. I've hurt people—my family, everyone I've come in contact with. I don't see any reason to live. I don't see how I could ever possibly forgive myself."

Her counselor listened, then replied, "Who did Jesus walk with on earth? If *he* can forgive you, then who are you not to forgive yourself?" WPM

I came not to call the righteous . . . ◆ Jesus

Forgiveness equals freedom.

John had one of those messy divorces. His wife did more than just leave him. In the process, she lied to the courts and took their son, disappearing whenever John had visitation. John was devastated. When the steel mill closed, he was forced to move out of state for work.

In the years that followed, he worked three jobs at a time in order to save enough money to return to court and see his son. Seven-day workweeks at sixteen hours a day damaged his health. In the end, through another series of lies, his wife managed to ban visitation forever. The overwork and grief took their toll; John's health broke down completely.

John had every reason to be angry with his ex-wife. He felt he had every reason to end his life as he intended. The bitterness took root and ate at what was left of his sweet nature.

He begged God to let him die. God refused. Instead, he sent John people who encouraged him to forgive his ex-wife. John was horrified. Forgive that beast? Never!

Eventually, he found he was praying God would help him to *want* to forgive her. Then he prayed he *would* forgive her. And finally, after several years, he found he prayed for her well-being.

By feeling and working through bitterness, anger, and depression, he learned that although his rage was valid, his resentments were hurting *him*. John found a freedom that opened doors to a whole new life. LHJ

> *Forgive us our trespasses,*
> *as we forgive those who trespass against us.*
> ◆ The Lord's Prayer

The world is unfair.

※ As long as the world is unfair, you have a reason to choose life.
Thelma and Louise knew about unfairness. In their cinematic world, rapists went free, lovers turned into abusers, and victims were severely punished. In the end, there was nothing left for them to do but drive over a cliff.

Or did they have another option? Could they have fought for justice? "Nobody would believe us," they said, and maybe they were right. Was that enough of a reason to give up?

In the nineteenth century Thelma and Louise might have identified with Elizabeth Packard. At the age of forty, Mrs. Packard's husband had her committed to the Illinois State Mental Hospital for daring to disagree with his theology. The hospital's superintendent, an influential physician, backed her husband. It appeared that Mrs. Packard's freedom was gone forever.

But Mrs. Packard chose to live.

During her three years in the hospital, she criticized the way the place was run and insisted upon patients' rights. This did not please the superintendent, so he labeled her incurable and discharged her to her husband's care. A few years later, her case came to trial: the jury immediately declared her sane. It took several more years to win back custody of her six children.

The world was unfair to Elizabeth Packard, so she went on the attack. Her books, articles, and lobbying efforts eventually changed several states' laws, making it much more difficult to have family members committed to mental institutions against their will. KLM

The only thing necessary for the triumph of evil is for good men to do nothing. ◆ Attributed to Edmund Burke

You won't really spare them pain.

The phone rang at two o'clock in the morning: a favorite uncle, my dad's brother, had died. A neighbor had found him in a local church, hanging from the rafters.

Devastated, we all asked *why?*

My uncle had watched my father die from cancer. Now my uncle thought his own cancer, in remission for several years, was recurring. Had he wanted to avoid suffering like my father?

My uncle had also been worried about his memory. His sister-in-law had Alzheimer's disease. Had he started to identify?

His wife knew his philosophy. "He said he never wanted to be a burden to me or the kids," she explained.

Not wanting to be a burden may seem unselfish. But is it really?

When a loved one commits suicide, the burden can be much greater than when a loved one dies in any other way. The greater burden is guilt, the continual musings of *what if?* and *if only* . . . There is also the burden of missed intimacy: of never being able to love in sickness as well as in health, of never sharing the pain.

To walk through the valley of the shadow together can be a growth experience of unparalleled proportions for both the sufferer and the ones who offer support. I wish I could have helped my uncle see this. For his sake. For ours, as his family. I wish he had let us share the burden. SF

When the business is done, there is sore havoc made in other people's lives, and a pin knocked out by which many subsidiary friendships hung together. There are empty chairs, solitary walks, and single beds at night. . . . In taking away our friends, death does not take them away utterly, but leaves behind a mocking, tragical, and soon intolerable residue, which must be hurriedly concealed.
◆ Robert Louis Stevenson, "Aes Triplex"

Suicide may not achieve the results you intended.

✳ Kathy was sixteen, unmarried, and thought she was pregnant. Her boyfriend ended the relationship, telling her he didn't love her.

Kathy swallowed a hundred aspirins, hoping to end her life.

Kathy *wasn't* pregnant, and she *didn't* die. She suffered miserably in the hospital for two days, and ruined the lining of her stomach.

Kathy is now eighteen. She has another boyfriend, plans for college, hopes for marriage and children of her own, and she has a stomach damaged for a lifetime.

Suicide may not bring about the results we intend.

There are too many unknowns.

"My husband of twelve years died," Kerry said, "and I wanted to kill myself, too. I didn't want to end my life; I just wanted to be with him more than I wanted to live in this world. But as I contemplated suicide, I wondered: What if I did kill myself and got to the other side? What if I got to Heaven and still had to be apart from him, until it was time for us to be together? What if I was simply trying to escape from dealing with pain and separation, and I would have to deal with it there anyway?

"I realized that there was no guarantee that suicide would really accomplish what I wanted," Kerry said. "So I didn't do it."

Brain damage from an unsuccessful overdose. Stomach problems. The mysterious questions of the afterlife, the world beyond—Heaven.

We don't know that suicide will bring about the desired results. It will certainly change our lives, but we cannot be certain how.
LHJ/KLM

If you can't change your circumstances, change the way you respond to them. ◆ Tim Hansel

You'll never know what could have been.

✳ "Dad and I went fishing together today. Not a big deal for most people. But for this father and son it was like a dream. I'm forty-two, and Dad is in his sixties. We haven't seen each other since I was four. He abandoned me. He left me so wounded I was unable to cope well as a child. In my early adult life I hit rock bottom. But there we were today, sitting in the middle of Lake Susan in a little rowboat. I loved it. *At least I would have loved it. They tell me that's what could have been.*"

• "After twelve painful years of trying to have children, we had given up. I was sure our problems stemmed from that abortion I'd had in high school. I'd never forgiven myself for it, and I finally fell apart. Then one day a miracle happened. A pregnant teenage girl called and said she wanted us to adopt her baby. Finally I was holding my own little girl. Oh, how I loved watching her grow. *At least I would have loved it. They tell me that's what could have been.*"

• "This picture I'm holding? It's my family, in front of our house. That cute little blond kid is my son. The beautiful woman is my wife. Me! The guy who lost everything a few years ago because cocaine became more important to me than my family, job, or house. It was all gone. Including my self-respect. Now I love my new family and my new life. *At least I would have loved it. They tell me that's what could have been.*"

We never really know what's coming—next year, next month, or even tomorrow. And we'll only find out if we wait around to see. CCD

What are some things you would like to see happen in your life? Write them down.

You may leave a legacy of suicide.

※ You have a dramatic impact on your children's lives—or deaths.

"Man is not made for defeat. . . . A man can be destroyed but not defeated." So wrote Ernest Hemingway in his classic novel, *The Old Man and the Sea.*

Within ten years of writing this Nobel Prize–winning tribute to an aging fisherman's endurance, Hemingway was dead by his own hand.

His father had committed suicide years earlier.

Hemingway's reasons for taking his own life were complex. He was ill, and he had been struggling with his writing. But clearly he had been deeply affected by his father's death.

Modern psychotherapy has verified the truth of the old adage, "Like father, like son." We know that people emulate their parents—even in actions that horrified them as children.

In a short story, Hemingway wrote: "His father had the finest pair of eyes he had ever seen and Nick had loved him very much and for a long time. Now, knowing how it had all been, even remembering the earliest times before things had gone badly was not good remembering. If he wrote it he could get rid of it."

Hemingway could never get rid of it.

You can give your children a gift that will last a lifetime: the belief that life, despite its raw edges, is worth living. LW

The value of life is not the end of it, but the use we make of it.
◆ Molière

You can find another way to make your point.

Joanie sat on the couch, watching Tom. "You simply don't care about what I want anymore," Joanie stated.

Joanie and Tom's marriage had been rocky for a while. Tom worked long hours at his demanding career. Joanie had frequent alcoholic binges. She wanted counseling, but Tom never had time.

Removing the lid from a bottle of sleeping pills, Joanie began taking one pill at a time. Her gaze never left Tom's face.

As the pills slid down Joanie's throat—one by one—Tom ran for the phone and called 911. Then he grabbed Joanie and forced her to swallow soapsuds, hoping that would make her throw up.

The soapsuds didn't work. Joanie had been drinking, which magnified the effect of the pills. The ambulance was slow in arriving.

Joanie wanted to make a point with Tom. She wanted to show him how much she hurt. She made that point. She also died.

We may be rageful with someone. We may hurt, then hurt more, because someone we love doesn't care how much we hurt. Threatening, or attempting, to end our life may seem to be a powerful way to make a point, to gain attention.

It is.

But there are other ways—ways that affirm, rather than destroy. And as much as we care about the other person, as much as we may believe they are causing our pain (and they may be), perhaps the person we really need to make the point with is ourself. Once we see and accept our own pain, we can begin to take creative, life-affirming steps to solve it. RW

Are you trying so desperately to make a point with someone that ending your life seems to be the only way to do it? What is the point? What are you trying to get this person to see? Talk to ten different people about it, then list five other life-affirming ways you could make that same point without destroying life.

You touch more lives than you know.

After centuries of neglect, we are just beginning to understand how fragile the environment is. We have learned that rain forests in Brazil and coastlines in Alaska affect the balance of the world.

We talk about ecosystems, realizing that the loss of one species threatens the existence of others.

People are the most important part of this ecosystem. Our lives are intertwined: visibly with our coworkers, neighbors, friends, family, and acquaintances; less visibly, with all who live.

We may have read about the "clustering" of suicides, particularly involving teenagers. One does it. Others follow.

An example has been set. A precedent. The act gathers strength from numbers. It becomes empowered.

But what we do also affects others in more far-reaching ways than we can see now—as we have learned from rain forests, coastlines, and oil spills. When we seek out the highest good for our life, we contribute to the good of humankind.

We set an example. A precedent. The act gathers strength from numbers. It becomes empowered. It spreads.

We help raise the consciousness and spirit of people—some we know, and many we don't. We become used by God to help transform the world. LW/MFB

Read Madeleine L'Engle's novel A Ring of Endless Light. *Many deaths occur in this book, but it shows how we are woven together in the tapestry of life.*

Your pain may reflect your joy.

✳ "Why don't you put her in a convalescent home?" a young man asked an elderly friend. John was seventy-five and cared for his seventy-year-old wife, a victim of Alzheimer's disease, at home.

Pensively John answered his friend's question: "Sometimes at night, while we lie in bed together and she's asleep, I just hold her and look at her. For a short time she's my wife again. She's how I remember her. It's worth all the frustration of the day."

I'm not saying, "Better to have loved and lost, than not to have loved at all." I'm saying: if you love, loss is part of that. If you live, your physical body wears out and you die. The world is not composed of opposites; life is composed of *wholes* that appear to be made up of opposites.

It's a package deal.

"If you move out to another human being, there is always the risk that that person will move away from you, leaving you more painfully alone than you were before. Love anything that lives—a person, a pet, a plant—and it will die. Trust anybody and you may be hurt; depend on anyone and that one may let you down," wrote M. Scott Peck in *The Road Less Traveled*. "The price of cathexis is pain. If someone is determined not to risk pain, then such a person must do without many things: having children, getting married, the ecstasy of sex, the hope of ambition, friendship—all that makes life alive, meaningful and significant. Move out or grow in any dimension and pain as well as joy will be your reward."
ERS/KLM

Today, God, help me hold a mirror up to my pain. I understand that my pain is real, but for a moment, let me dwell on the joy that it reflects.

God is there to catch us.

✳ Marty is a single parent, works two jobs, is raising three small children in a new town, and has no friends or family to confide in. After a frightening experience one evening, when she seriously considered ending her own life, she sought help.

She's now building a support network that can help make what she's been facing alone easier to handle.

Has anyone ever told you that life or God won't give you more than you can handle? Did you want to lash out at them, and say, "Honey, I've got more than I can handle right now"?

"Each time someone tells me that 'God won't let me be tempted beyond what I'm able,' another major crisis shoves me over the emotional cliff," said Betsy. "When I've been betrayed, I haven't been tempted; I've been severely wounded. When I've lost my job for the fourth time, I haven't been tempted; I've been devastated!

"I think life gives us more than we can handle. But if we let him, God will be there to catch us when we fall over the edge of the cliff. He won't let us be destroyed. What I need to hear most when I've been pushed over the cliff is that maybe life will give me more than I can handle, but God will go through it with me when it happens."

If you're falling over the edge of the cliff, you don't have to destroy yourself. Let yourself fall into a net of support. LHJ/TB

What is grace? I know until you ask me; when you ask me, I do not know. ◆ Saint Augustine

You may be surprised by what happens next.

As world events unfold at breakneck speed, you may want to see what the future holds.

Suicide rates decrease in countries undergoing revolution. People seem to have an innate desire to find out what will happen next.

Storytellers discovered this long ago. You'll recall that in the *Arabian Nights* the sultan of India killed each of his wives after their wedding night. But the clever Scheherazade saved herself by telling him a story that stretched for one thousand and one consecutive nights. She kept him hooked for so long by always stopping at a suspenseful moment. Each story was a cliff-hanger. By the time of the conclusion, he was in love with her.

Real life also has its cliff-hangers. Those who followed recent events in the Soviet Union were caught up in a story as dramatic and exciting as any work of fiction.

The fall of the Berlin Wall, the apparent end of the Cold War, the allied victory in Operation Desert Storm, the dismantling of the Communist party and the Soviet Union—who would have predicted these events five years ago?

Someday, perhaps, we will see democracy across the globe and the end of armed conflict between nations. Overly optimistic, you say?

You'll never know if you don't stick around. LW

> *Grow old along with me!*
> *The best is yet to be,*
> *The last of life, for which the first was made.*
> *Our times are in His hand*
> *Who saith, "A whole I planned,*
> *Youth shows but half; trust God: see all nor be afraid!"*
> ◆ Robert Browning, "Rabbi Ben Ezra"

Today is a gift.

✳ When doctors told Orville Kelly he had terminal cancer, he felt life could not be more unfair. He was only forty-two, attended church regularly, and had a wife and four children. Frightened, he contemplated suicide. But he didn't really want to die. He wanted to find a way to live.

One day while driving home from a chemotherapy session with his wife, Orville turned to her and said, "Let's not talk about it. I'm going to die from cancer unless something else kills me first, but I'm not dead yet. So let's start enjoying life again. Let's go home tonight and have a barbecue, just like old times."

Orville had decided to accept each day as a gift from God. His changed attitude encouraged his family and strengthened them throughout his remaining seven years. "After all, none of us really knows when he is going to die," Kelly commented in his book, *Until Tomorrow Comes*. "We are all terminal, in a sense."

Orville's manner of coping was to begin each day "not as another day closer to death, but as another day of life. I accept each day as a gift from God to be appreciated, enjoyed, and lived to its fullest." AEH

> *This is the day that the Lord has made;*
> *let us rejoice and be glad in it.*
> ◆ Psalm 118

Life is a journey.

There is a forest, dark and deep—the forest through which I've come. I thought it would be beautiful. I had heard stories that it was. People who'd been there talked of streams of laughter, meadows of peace, pools of nurture, and waterfalls of joy.

I found rivers of hatred, swamps of ridicule and abuse. I found brambles and snares of denial and hopelessness.

After many years, I escaped to a clearing. The gentle breeze pushed away the old things and cleansed me. I drank in the fragrance of hope and saw with new eyes the beauty around me. I held the distant rainbow in the palm of my hand, and strength soared through me.

But the respite didn't last long. I gathered up my possessions and began a new journey into the new forest.

The outer forest is lush and full of the things I've heard about and wanted. The people I meet are affectionate and joyous. But I fear the uncertainty of what lies ahead. Is this forest going to be the same as the other? Is this only another trap? A party before the funeral?

I look back and see a signpost I hadn't noticed before. Pointing to the way I've come, it says, "No longer an option." Pointing to the path I now take, it says, "Your life."

I hoist my knapsack and grip my walking stick. And I begin my journey once again. LHJ

In the middle of the journey of our life I came to myself within a dark wood where the straight way was lost. ♦ Dante, *The Divine Comedy*

CHAPTER SIX

Finding Your Wings

W hat kind of bird would you want to be?" Shane asked me one day.

"I don't know," I said. "Maybe a cardinal?"

"No, Mom," he said back. "An eagle!"

Caterpillars are not born to be caterpillars. They're baby butterflies that look entirely different from what they're eventually going to be. They live their life as caterpillars, crawling around on the ground and in trees. Then one day, a cocoon forms around them. It happens naturally, when it's time. For a while, they live in darkness, in a place totally different from the places they lived before.

They are being transformed into butterflies. That transformation is powerful—unlike anything they've known. *It takes a change of this magnitude to make a caterpillar into a butterfly.*

Often those dark places in life—those places so dark that we lose hope and want our life to be over—are times of deep transformation. We are being changed at levels we cannot imagine. The times of greatest pain in our lives often reflect those times of great transformation. We don't have to be in pain to be changed, but sometimes we are.

Sometimes that transformation is so great as to include the experience we call death—the shedding of our physical body. Sometimes someone we love very much dies.

Or we may get stopped in our tracks by financial disaster, an addiction, another person's addiction, losing a job, being rejected or betrayed by someone we love.

For some reason, life as we have known it changes—sometimes in an instant. And we lose hope. We lose hope for life as we have known it because our life is being transformed into something beyond what we could hope for or imagine.

I've also learned that the more I resist change—and my feelings—the more and longer it hurts. There comes a time to surrender to the darkness—so light can come again.

When I was in the process of decorating my home, I told my decorator I wanted a special picture in the entrance hallway—a cross, some picture representing my faith. Several weeks later, she came back with one portraying Jesus, dead, on the cross.

I looked at it, then said no. I don't want a picture of a dead Jesus in my house. *Tell me about the resurrection.*

There's a higher purpose for our lives, a plan that we can't see right now. And it's OK to trust that purpose and plan—even if we don't see it clearly or fully understand it. Or even like it that much.

I don't believe we were intended to slug around on the ground, carrying a heavy burden on our backs.

We're meant to claim our wings and fly. Sometimes, to get our wings strong enough to fly, we have to beat on the edges of our cocoon for a while. It hurts, too. But the pain isn't the purpose; it's just sometimes part of the path.

Live in the present moment. As gracefully as possible, let go of moments past. Feel and release your fears, too.

Then, learn to fly. Trust the butterfly that will come out of the cocoon.

Better yet, become an eagle. And teach others how to fly, too.

God bless, as you discover your *reason to live.*

RESOURCES

What to do if you are alone and thinking about suicide

- ◆ Sit down and breathe deeply. Breathe deeply again and again.
- ◆ Turn on the lights or open a door or window.
- ◆ Pick up the phone and call a friend, even if you have to call collect. Talk to the operator if you don't have strength to dial the number.
- ◆ Say your name out loud. Say your friends' names out loud. Repeat and combine these names with your name.
- ◆ Cry, even if it means weeping bitterly. Scream: "God, why am I in such despair? Why did you do this to me? Tell me why."
- ◆ Pray. Say: "God, help me. Please give me a reason to live."
- ◆ Touch yourself. Feel the rapid beating of your heart.
- ◆ Turn on the television, radio, or stereo.
- ◆ Close your eyes and think about *The Wizard of Oz* or chocolate ice cream or giraffes.
- ◆ Get out a photo album and look at pictures of your family and friends.

◆ If you have a pet, pick it up and hold it tightly.

◆ When you have the strength, get out from where you are. Go to the movies. Go to the shopping mall. Go to a neighbor's or a friend's house. If you are afraid to drive, run as fast as you can for as long as you can. Get yourself to where there are people.

SJA

What to do when someone says, "I'm going to kill myself"

◆ Accept what is said and treat it seriously.

◆ Listen, even if the person is verbally abusing you. Say: "I'm sorry you are in so much pain" or "I will not abandon you."

◆ Embrace or touch the person. Rub his or her back.

◆ Do not give advice and do not say, "Everything will be all right." Say: "I'm asking you not to kill yourself. Please do not kill yourself. My heart will break if you kill yourself."

◆ Do not debate whether suicide is right or wrong. Do not add to the person's guilt by saying, "How can you face God? Think how your parents and friends would feel! How can you be so selfish?"

◆ Call the police if the situation is immediately life-threatening.

◆ Do not leave the person alone if you believe the risk of suicide is immediate. Trust your suspicions that the person may be self-destructive.

◆ Do not swear you will keep the person's intentions a secret. You may lose a friend, but you may save a life.

◆ Help the person recall how he or she used to cope. Ask what the person needs most right now. Food? Sleep? Money? A hug? Answers? Talk freely about the person's intentions. Try to determine whether the person has a plan for suicide—the more detailed the plan, the greater the risk.

◆ Pray for the person silently, saying: "God, you are the source of life. Please graft onto this person's heart a reason to live."

SJA

Do you or does someone you know want to die?

Answer these questions for yourself or the hurting person you care about:

◆ Have you recently withdrawn from therapeutic help because it's just not worth it and it will never really make a difference?

◆ Have you been abusing drugs or alcohol lately in order to render yourself immune to an overwhelming feeling of despair?

◆ Is there a history of suicide in your family? Do you feel that "the sins of the fathers" have fallen on your shoulders and that killing yourself is the only way to eradicate this cancer in your family once and for all?

◆ Are you using a lot of profanity? Are you yelling at people you love? Are you driving your car at high rates of speed, sometimes thinking about how easy it would be to drift into the path of an oncoming truck?

◆ Have you stopped washing your clothes or the dishes? Do you leave bills unopened? Do you look disheveled? Are you showering only once a week?

◆ Have you stopped going to classes? Did you purposely forget about an important meeting or a final exam, figuring it didn't matter?

◆ Have you threatened suicide? Have you said or written in a letter or poem that you wish you were dead?

◆ Do you hear your own voice in "death literature" by writers such as Sylvia Plath or Anne Sexton? Do you imagine your own funeral and what your friends will say when they see your body lying in a casket?

◆ Have you attempted suicide before—even if you only wanted attention and knew you weren't going to die?

◆ Do you spend a lot of time by yourself? Alone in bed? Are your friends exasperated by your mood swings?

◆ Have you thought about the different ways to kill yourself? Have you thought about where you can find a gun or other weapon? Have you counted the pills in the medicine cabinet?

◆ Have you gone through all of your possessions and labeled them so they would go to the right person after you are gone? Have you begun giving friends your most prized possessions? Have you closed your bank accounts? Have you suddenly stopped talking or writing about death? Do you feel like death is controlling you? Have you written a suicide note?

SJA

Emergency phone numbers

✴ Phone numbers change often, and not all 800 numbers are available everywhere. If the number listed here does not work for you, call 1-800-555-1212 for directory assistance.

Emergency 911
Suicide Prevention Hotline 1-800-333-4444
Suicide Prevention Hotline 1-800-882-3386

Adcare Referral (drug and alcohol problems) 1-800-252-6465
AIDS Clinical Trials Information Service
   (Hearing impaired) 1-800-243-7012
AIDS Clinical Trials Information Service 1-800-TRIALS-A
Alzheimer's Association 1-800-572-6037
Association for Experiential Education
   (Colorado) 303-492-1547
Befrienders Ministry . . . . 1-800-328-6819, ext. 5095
Big Brothers and Big Sisters (Pennsylvania) 215-567-7000
Catholic Charities (DC) 202-639-8400
Child Abuse Hotline 1-800-421-0353
Childhelp USA Child Abuse Hotline 1-800-422-4453
Christian Camping International (Illinois) 708-462-0300
Cocaine Hotline 1-800-COCAINE
Consumer Credit Counseling Services 1-800-388-2227
Golden Valley Treatment Centers 1-800-321-2273
Grief Recovery Institute (California) 213-650-1234
Habitat for Humanity (Georgia) 912-924-6935
Hearing Aid Helpline 1-800-521-5247
Literacy Volunteers of America (New York) 315-445-8000
Mothers Against Drunk Driving (MADD) 1-800-253-MADD
National AIDS Information Clearinghouse 1-800-458-5231
National AIDS Network (DC) 202-293-2437

National Coalition Against Child Abuse (Illinois) . . 312-663-3520
National Coalition for the Homeless (DC) 202-659-3310
National HIV and AIDS Information Service Hotline
   (English) 1-800-342-AIDS
National HIV and AIDS Information Service Hotline
   (Hearing impaired) 1-800-AIDS-TTY
National HIV and AIDS Information Service Hotline
   (Spanish) 1-800-344-SIDA
National Hospice Organization (Virginia) 703-243-5900
National Institute of Health Information on AIDS
   Drug Studies 1-800-AIDS-NIH
National Institute on Drug and Alcohol Abuse 1-800-HELP
National Outdoor Leadership School (Wyoming) . . 307-332-6973
National Runaway Switchboard 1-800-621-4000
National Self-Help Clearinghouse (New York) 212-642-2944
National Sexually Transmitted Diseases Hotline . . 1-800-227-8922
New Life Treatment Center Adolescent
   Wilderness Program 1-800-332-TEEN
New Life Treatment Centers 1-800-227-LIFE
Outward Bound 1-800-882-8923
Parents Against Cancer Together 1-800-962-4748
Parents Anonymous 1-800-421-0353
People with AIDS Coalition (New York) 212-532-0290
People with AIDS Coalition hotline (New York) . . . 1-800-828-3280
Pets Are Wonderful Support (California) 415-824-4040
Recording for the Blind (New Jersey) 609-452-0606
Samaritans (New York) 212-677-3009
Summit Adventures 1-800-827-1282
United Way (Virginia) 703-836-7100
Volunteers in Service to America
   (VISTA, the domestic Peace Corps) (DC) 202-634-9445

Our reasons for living are not, by any means, all-inclusive. They are simply reasons we have gathered from some people around the country. We want to understand more about why people choose life. You can help us! If you have considered suicide and chosen life, please write us a letter and tell us your reason to live.

Melody Beattie and the editors
c/o Tyndale House Publishers, Inc.
P.O. Box 80
Wheaton, IL 60189-0080